T0363079

MADE FOR BEGINNERS
+ EXPERIENCED ANGLERS

TICAL WINCHING POWER
JRATE **CASTS** | **BIG RANGE**

3LEMS! WWW.ALVEY.COM.AU

CONTENTS

DEDICATION

This book is dedicated to my wife Leanne and our two great kids Chris and Alissa who put up with our study and garage looking like a small tackle shop, the hours that I spend on the water trying to perfect the art of fishing and the long hours that I spend in front of the computer putting articles and books together for other anglers to read and learn from.

It is also dedicated to all the anglers I have had the pleasure to fish with over the years and who have also taught me many different fishing techniques. Like they always say, "you are never too old to learn".

I would also like to dedicate this book to Pure Fishing Australia, Pflueger, Tackle Tactics and Ugly Fish Sun glasses. It is through their support over the years that I have been able to put together books like this one. Thank you so much.

First published 2013,
Reprinted 2015, 2020

Published and distributed by
AFN Fishing & Outdoors
PO Box 544 Croydon, Victoria 3136
Telephone: (03) 9729 8788 Facsimile: (03) 9729 7833
Email: sales@afn.com.au
Website: www.afn.com.au

©Australian Fishing Network 2020

ISBN: 9781 8651 3232 7

Printed in China

Gary Brown is what most people would call a "fishing nut", he lives for it. His passion for fishing and all things marine shows through in the quality of his publications and his ability to transfer long and hard earned knowledge to those who need to get it in quick time. Gary may be a fisherman of high standing, but first and foremost he is a teacher.

The knowledge stored away in Gary's being has been hard won and taken some 40 plus years to garner. That knowledge has been gainfully passed on in books, magazine articles, fishing club or store talk nights and at many fishing tournaments. GB is always one to watch for in a fishing competition as he knows better than the back of his hand most of, if not all the productive spots in the coastal waterways, off the best wharves and jetty's and the rock and beach locations of NSW.

And that brings me to this publication.

In these days of "on line" fast tracked, force fed information overload, Gary has taken the time to sit back, think about what an angler needs and transfer that into an easily read and understood package that any angler, whether hard core or just beginning, can use to their advantage. Within the pages of Landbased Fishing Spots for Sydney Harbour, things like seasonal species variation, tides, best species to target, suitable rigs and even the closest amenities for those family days and much more can be found for your favourite Sydney harbour spot. By using this guide and the friendly sales assistant at your favoured tackle outlet, better catches and an understanding of why fishing is such a great pastime for you and the family will follow.

If you bump into Gary on one of your days on the water, say g'day, he loves a chat and you just might get that "secret spot" from him.

Tight lines
John Bell

SAFETY MESSAGE

Consideration for others and always think of safety first. No fish is worth your life.

You may not think that fishing from the shore can be dangerous, but it can. It doesn't take much to trip and fall while going down a set of stairs or track to a new found fishing spot. So care needs to be taken at all times. Wear the correct footwear, take a torch during your night-time sojourns and don't be in such a rush.

In this book there are a number of places where you have to park near private residences. Make sure that you treat them with respect, don't make unnecessary noise and never leave your garbage behind.

When fishing off the ocean rocks you will need to keep an eye on the swell. It would be a good idea to never fish alone and always wear a life jacket. Once again wearing the correct footwear is essential. Even though fishing off the beach seems very safe you will need to keep an eye on those shifting sand bars.

My say

I started fishing back in the early sixties from the shore in Botany Bay and the Georges River for bream, flathead, luderick and whiting, progressing to the Port Hacking and Woronora Rivers, adding leatherjackets, crabs, tailor, mullet and mulloway to the list.

I have fished off the beaches since I was 10 and the rocks since I was 14 and over the years I have travelled around the coastline of Australia fishing in both very populated and remote areas. In those early years most of my beach and rock fishing was concentrated from Palm Beach to Stanwell Park in Sydney and from Wollongong to Seven Mile Beach at Gerroa on the south coast.

At 21, I felt the urge to explore other fishing places around Australia, so in 1975 I found myself in Western Australia fishing beaches and rock platforms from Yanchep, just north of Perth to Margaret River down south. While in the west I also fished some of the remote beaches from Cape Freycinet to Albany. On my way back to the east coast of Australia I fished at places such as Ceduna, Portland, Barwon Heads, Wilson's Promontory and Mallacoota.

I have lived in the southern area of Sydney for 33 years working in the construction field in NSW as a teacher and manager of the Commercial and Industrial section of NSW TAFE. Whilst working for TAFE, I have continued to fish and have developed, written and taught a course on recreational fishing. This course is now a Certificate 3 in Recreational Fishing and is currently being taught by other teachers in various states and territories of Australia.

In my spare time I have started up fishing classes and talks in various bait and tackle shops throughout the Sydney region, namely Amazon Tackle at Wetherill Park, Windybanks Bait and Tackle at Mount Colah and a number of BCF stores throughout NSW. I also give fishing and tackle talks to around 6 fishing clubs throughout the year.

I wrote my first book for Australian Fishing Network (AFN), *Fishing Guide to Sydney and Hawkesbury Waterways* in 2002. In 2005 I again wrote a book for AFN, *How to fish the Beaches and Rocks of Australia*. In 2010 I put together the *South of Sydney to Batemans Bay* book of fishing spots and in 2011 *How to Catch Australia's Favourite Saltwater Fish*.

Together with with Scotty Lyons from Southern Sydney Fishing Tours I have produced two DVDs, *A Day on the Bay* and *Port Hacking – The Jewel of the South*. Currently I contribute to weekly and monthly reports, fishing and boating articles, and area guides for a number of state and national fishing and boating magazines and web sites.

It's not for everyone, but one thing I can't seem to get enough of is competing in the catch and release bream and flathead tournaments. Over the years I have been able to learn so much from anglers competing in these tournament.

Then there is the added bonus of the friends and mates I have made during those competitions over the years.

Gary Brown

SYDNEY AREA LOCATION MAP

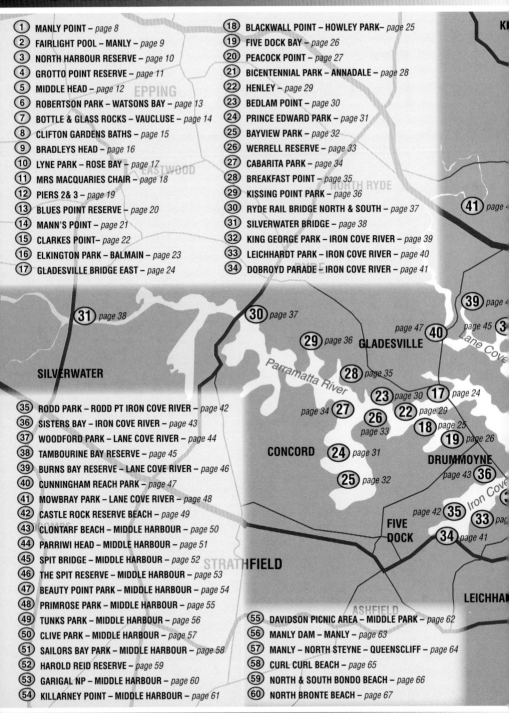

1. MANLY POINT – *page 8*
2. FAIRLIGHT POOL – MANLY – *page 9*
3. NORTH HARBOUR RESERVE – *page 10*
4. GROTTO POINT RESERVE – *page 11*
5. MIDDLE HEAD – *page 12*
6. ROBERTSON PARK – WATSONS BAY – *page 13*
7. BOTTLE & GLASS ROCKS – VAUCLUSE – *page 14*
8. CLIFTON GARDENS BATHS – *page 15*
9. BRADLEYS HEAD – *page 16*
10. LYNE PARK – ROSE BAY – *page 17*
11. MRS MACQUARIES CHAIR – *page 18*
12. PIERS 2& 3 – *page 19*
13. BLUES POINT RESERVE – *page 20*
14. MANN'S POINT – *page 21*
15. CLARKES POINT– *page 22*
16. ELKINGTON PARK – BALMAIN – *page 23*
17. GLADESVILLE BRIDGE EAST – *page 24*

18. BLACKWALL POINT – HOWLEY PARK– *page 25*
19. FIVE DOCK BAY – *page 26*
20. PEACOCK POINT – *page 27*
21. BICENTENNIAL PARK – ANNADALE – *page 28*
22. HENLEY – *page 29*
23. BEDLAM POINT – *page 30*
24. PRINCE EDWARD PARK – *page 31*
25. BAYVIEW PARK – *page 32*
26. WERRELL RESERVE – *page 33*
27. CABARITA PARK – *page 34*
28. BREAKFAST POINT – *page 35*
29. KISSING POINT PARK – *page 36*
30. RYDE RAIL BRIDGE NORTH & SOUTH – *page 37*
31. SILVERWATER BRIDGE – *page 38*
32. KING GEORGE PARK – IRON COVE RIVER – *page 39*
33. LEICHHARDT PARK – IRON COVE RIVER – *page 40*
34. DOBROYD PARADE – IRON COVE RIVER – *page 41*

41. *page*

31. *page 38*
30. *page 37*
29. *page 36*
28. *page 35*
39. *page*
40. *page 47*
page 45
3
GLADESVILLE
Lane Cove

SILVERWATER
Parramatta River

23. *page 30*
17. *page 24*
27. *page 34*
26. *page 33*
22. *page 29*
18. *page 25*
19. *page 26*
24. *page 31*
25. *page 32*
CONCORD
DRUMMOYNE
36. *page 43*

35. RODD PARK – RODD PT IRON COVE RIVER – *page 42*
36. SISTERS BAY – IRON COVE RIVER – *page 43*
37. WOODFORD PARK – LANE COVE RIVER – *page 44*
38. TAMBOURINE BAY RESERVE – *page 45*
39. BURNS BAY RESERVE – LANE COVE RIVER – *page 46*
40. CUNNINGHAM REACH PARK – *page 47*
41. MOWBRAY PARK – LANE COVE RIVER – *page 48*
42. CASTLE ROCK RESERVE BEACH – *page 49*
43. CLONTARF BEACH – MIDDLE HARBOUR – *page 50*
44. PARRIWI HEAD – MIDDLE HARBOUR – *page 51*
45. SPIT BRIDGE – MIDDLE HARBOUR – *page 52*
46. THE SPIT RESERVE – MIDDLE HARBOUR – *page 53*
47. BEAUTY POINT PARK – MIDDLE HARBOUR – *page 54*
48. PRIMROSE PARK – MIDDLE HARBOUR – *page 55*
49. TUNKS PARK – MIDDLE HARBOUR – *page 56*
50. CLIVE PARK – MIDDLE HARBOUR – *page 57*
51. SAILORS BAY PARK – MIDDLE HARBOUR – *page 58*
52. HAROLD REID RESERVE – *page 59*
53. GARIGAL NP – MIDDLE HARBOUR – *page 60*
54. KILLARNEY POINT – MIDDLE HARBOUR – *page 61*

35. *page 42*
33. *pa*
34. *page 41*
FIVE DOCK
Iron Cove
STRATHFIELD
LEICHHA

55. DAVIDSON PICNIC AREA – MIDDLE PARK – *page 62*
56. MANLY DAM – MANLY – *page 63*
57. MANLY – NORTH STEYNE – QUEENSCLIFF – *page 64*
58. CURL CURL BEACH – *page 65*
59. NORTH & SOUTH BONDO BEACH – *page 66*
60. NORTH BRONTE BEACH – *page 67*

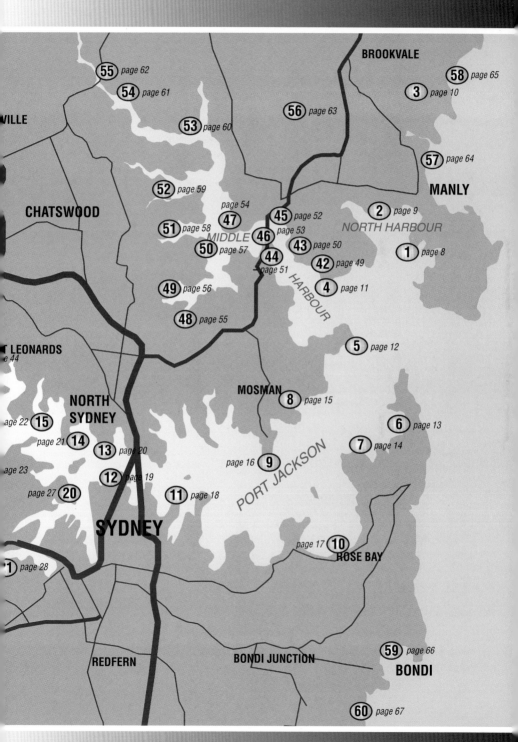

BROOKVALE

55 *page 62*

54 *page 61*

53 *page 60*

56 *page 63*

58 *page 65*

3 *page 10*

VILLE

57 *page 64*

52 *page 59*

MANLY

CHATSWOOD

page 54

47

2 *page 9*

45 *page 52*

NORTH HARBOUR

51 *page 58*

46 *page 53*

1 *page 8*

50 *page 57*

MIDDLE

43 *page 50*

44 *page 51*

42 *page 49*

49 *page 56*

HARBOUR

4 *page 11*

48 *page 55*

LEONARDS
e 44

5 *page 12*

MOSMAN

8 *page 15*

NORTH
SYDNEY

age 22 15

page 21 14

13 *page 20*

6 *page 13*

7 *page 14*

age 23

12 *page 19*

page 16 9

page 27 20

11 *page 18*

PORT JACKSON

SYDNEY

page 17 10

1 *page 28*

ROSE BAY

REDFERN

BONDI JUNCTION

59 *page 66*

BONDI

60 *page 67*

MANLY POINT

🔍 HOW TO GET THERE

Once you are on the Esplanade, turn left into Stuart Street, find a parking spot and walk down to the boat ramp at the end of Craig Avenue. Then just walk around the foreshore to the point.

🔍 SNAPSHOT

PLATFORM
HARBOUR ROCKS

TARGET FISH
BREAM
DUSKY FLATHEAD
SAND WHITING
TAILOR
SALMON
LUDERICK
LEATHERJACKET
YELLOWTAIL
SILVER TREVALLY
SQUID
FLOUNDER

BEST BAIT
WHOLE/HALF PILCHARDS
SQUID
PRAWN
MULLET
TUNA
BONITO

BEST LURES
METAL SLICES &
POPPERS

BEST TIMES
RISING TIDE

SEASONS
Bream **February to May**

Dusky flathead
November to April

Sand whiting
October to April

Silver trevally
March to June

Flounder
November to April

Salmon **March to June**

Tailor **March to August**

Luderick
March to September

Leatherjacket, yellowtail
& squid **Year round**

The car parking at Manly Point is a pain, but it is definitely worth the walk to the reserve at the end of Addison Road and down.

You could always try Little Manly Point or the beach on either side for bream, whiting and trevally.

Manly Point juts out into Manly Cove and is a fairly protected spot from any swell that may come in through the harbour entrance when the seas are big outside. Even though this area is not classed as ocean rocks you will need to take care when fishing from here, especially when there are big seas running from the south. The point is a great spot to fish from during the warmer months of the year when the nor-easters are blowing as this spot is fairly protected from these winds. The bottom here is a mixture of sand, boulders and broken shells.

TACTICS
Surf outfits are recommended enabling long casts to reach the deeper water. Due to the large amount of rocks in the area, snagging up is almost impossible to avoid. With this in mind, anglers should take a back-up of rigs. When targeting the species listed under 'Target Fish', a paternoster rig tied from 15 lb trace will suffice. The hook size however, will differ from species to species with a long shank size 6 for sweep and trevally and a bait holder size 1/0 for the salmon. These species are best targeted when the tide is low. This will allow anglers to walk onto the rocks to further their casts. Ideally, berley is the most effective method used to attract fish to the area.

BAITS AND LURES
Try using whole pilchards for the salmon and tailor, strips of mullet, tuna and bonito for the bream and silver trevally. In saying that, peeled prawns will catch almost anything that can be caught here. When I fish here I take a bucket of chicken layer pellets or a bag of bread for berley. Forty to 70 g metal slices and slugs will get the required distance when casting for salmon and tailor. You could also try casting out large surface poppers before working them back towards the shore.

BEST TIDE/TIMES
I have found that the last two hours of the rising tide and the first two hours of the falling tide produce the best results. This can be a great spot to fish during those north-east blows during the summer months.

AMENITIES
The closest amenities would be back at the Manly Pier.

KIDS AND FAMILIES
Not a real good place to take the kids as it is a fairly hard walk in from the parking spaces. Maybe try the beach back further in the bay.

FINALLY
A very popular location for surfers and anglers alike. Fish the tides stated above for best results.

FAIRLIGHT POOL — MANLY

HOW TO GET THERE

Once you are on Lauderale Avenue at Manly, turn into Fairlight Crescent. From here it is a short walk to the Esplanade Scenic walkway where you will see Fairlight Pool.

SNAPSHOT

PLATFORM
ESTUARY ROCKS

TARGET FISH
BREAM
DUSKY FLATHEAD
SAND WHITING
LEATHERJACKET
SLIMY MACKEREL
YELLOWTAIL
SILVER TREVALLY
LUDERICK
SQUID
FLOUNDER

BEST BAIT
PRAWNS
BLOOD AND BEACH WORMS
WHOLE AND HALF PILCHARDS
GREEN WEED
CABBAGE

BEST LURES
METAL LURES

BEST TIMES
RUN OUT TIDE

Great place to fish for bream trevally and whiting close to the pool. Further out on to the point you will find deep water for leatherjackets, flounder and squid.

You will find that the parking here is very limited, so to get a spot you may have to park a couple of streets away. There is a set of swimming baths adjacent to the waters, and from here it is a short walk to the water's edge. A good set of polarised sunglasses will be a great asset when fishing this area. If you are going to fish light you will need them to locate the sandy patches between the reefs. For those of you with larger rods you will need to be able to cast about 30 to 40 m to get over the rock shelf.

TACTICS

The main fish species you will catch here are bream, squid, luderick, silver trevally and leatherjacket and they are best targeted with light to medium outfits. For the leatherjacket you will need to use a single hooked paternoster rig with a small snapper sinker. The best hook sizes are number 10 to 12 long shanks and the bait I would suggest to use is small strips of squid or small pieces of prawn. You want just enough to cover the bend of the hook. A rising tide that occurs in the latter part of the day seems to produce more fish here. For the bream and silver trevally you will need to either fish as light as possible (ball sinker down onto the bait) or use a small bobby cork and the rod will need to be between 3 and 6 kg with either a 40 to 50 sized threadline reel or a 15 cm Alvey side cast reel. You could try fishing out wider here, but you will need to put in a rather large cast of somewhere near 40 to 50 metres.

BAITS AND LURES

Prawns, blood, tube and beach worms, pink nippers and peeled prawns are the go for the bream and silver trevally. You could also try suspending a whole pilchard under a bobby cork. For the luderick you will need to find yourself either some green weed or cabbage for bait. It is also a great idea to have enough cabbage or weed so that you can chop it up and mix it with sand for berley.

BEST TIDE/TIMES

The run-out tide seems to produce the better catches of bream, silver trevally and whiting. The last part of the rising tide is most productive when targeting flathead. When chasing squid it doesn't seem to matter as long as the water is fairly clear and the sun is low in the sky.

AMENITIES

The closest amenities would be back at the Manly Pier.

KIDS AND FAMILIES

Fairlight Pool Manly, is a great place to take the family. Depending on how good they are at casting you may have to cast for them so that the bait reaches the sandy spots.

SEASONS

Bream
February to May

Dusky flathead
November to April

Sand whiting
October to April

Silver trevally & slimy mackerel
March to June

Luderick
March to September

Leatherjacket, Yellowtail & Squid
Year round

NORTH HARBOUR RESERVE

🔍 HOW TO GET THERE

Travel east along Sydney Road, Balgowlah, and turn right at Condamine Street then head south until you come to North Harbour Reserve on the left. Park your car and walk through the park until you find the breakwall at the water's edge

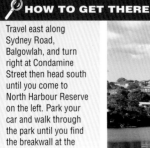

At low tide you can walk out onto the sand spit here and fish in the deeper water.

🔍 SNAPSHOT

Platform
SMALL BREAK WALL, CONCRETE PATH.

Target species
BREAM
DUSKY FLATHEAD
SAND WHITING
LEATHERJACKET
YELLOWTAIL
SILVER TREVALLY
PAN SIZE SNAPPER
SQUID
FLOUNDER

Best bait
PRAWNS
MULLET STRIPS

Best lures
SOFT PLASTICS
SHALLOW DIVING LURES

Best time
HIGH TIDE

RIGHT: *Due to the number of people who walk along here I would suggest that you make yourself fairly mobile and work the whole walk.*

The reserve is an ideal spot for picnics and BBQs as well as functions and weddings. It includes two double electric BBQs, seating and tables, large trees that provide plenty of shade as well as plenty of grassed area. Right across the road is a small kiosk for ice creams, snacks and coffee. For children, the reserve offers a shaded playground, half basketball court and a small skateboard, scooter, bike track around the play area.

TACTICS
A small ball sinker straight down onto the hook would be ideal here when using peeled prawns, worms, pink nippers and strips of mullet or tuna. Cast out as far as you can and then set the rod between one of the boulders on the rock wall. Either use a bait feeder reel or leave the bail arm open and wait for the fish to take off. If you're going to use soft plastics or hardbodied lures I would suggest that you fish as light as possible. Pick a spot and cast out in an umbrella shape. If nothing takes the lure, move about 20 m to either the left or right and repeat the process over again. This will allow you to cover a fair bit of ground.

BAITS AND LURES
This would be a good spot to come and try out those soft plastics and shallow diving lures for bream, flathead and whiting. The drop off at low tide would be a place to try soft plastics on either 1/4th or 3/8th oz jigheads.

SEASONS

Bream
February to May

Dusky flathead
November to April

Sand whiting
October to April

Silver trevally
March to June

Leatherjacket, Yellowtail & Squid
Year round

BEST TIDE/TIMES
This is definitely a high tide spot as the area is very shallow. You could walk out on the sand bar at low tide though and fish off the edge of the drop off in much deeper water. Early morning and late afternoons seem to produce the better catches.

AMENITIES
Playground, café/kiosk, scooter track for young kids, basketball court, toilets, BBQs, picnic areas, seating, shade.

KIDS AND FAMILIES
Great place to bring the kids as you don't need to cast too far. There is a park with swings, picnic tables and there is also a nearby shop for a coffee or an ice cream.

GROTTO POINT RESERVE

ABOVE: *Best fished during calm seas.*

LEFT: *Dart are not a frequent visitor to Grotto Point, but if you berley you may be surprised what you catch.*

HOW TO GET THERE

Travel south along Woodland Street at Balgowlah Heights, left into Alder Street left again into Cutler Street. Park then walk about 30 to 40 minutes out to Grotto Point.

SNAPSHOT

Platform
HARBOUR ROCKS

Target species
BREAM, DUSKY FLATHEAD, SAND WHITING, LEATHERJACKETS, YELLOWTAIL, SILVER TREVALLY, PAN SIZE SNAPPER, TAILOR, AUSTRALIAN SALMON, SQUID, KINGFISH, FLOUNDER

Best baits
TUNA, BONITO, MULLET, PILCHARDS, PRAWNS

Best lures
METAL SLICES, POPPERS, & SOFT PLASTICS

Best time
HIGH TIDE ON EITHER THE RUN-IN OR RUN-OUT TIDES.

SEASONS

Bream **February to May**

Dusky flathead **November to April**

Sand whiting **October to April**

Pan sized snapper **Winter**

Silver trevally & salmon **March to June**

Flounder **November to April**

Tailor **March to August**

Kingfish **November to May**

Leatherjacket, yellowtail & squid **Year round**

Grotto Point Reserve is situated in the Sydney Harbour National Park and it features a number of superb swimming spots, bush walking tracks, picnic areas, as well as a great fishing spot at Grotto Point. The walk out to Grotto Point boasts magnificent views above the entrance to Middle Harbour and the walk provides plenty of views of Middle Head and Sydney Harbour.

TACTICS
Luderick have been known to frequent this stretch of water during autumn to winter. You can use either a stemmed float or a bobby cork here, but you will need to set the rig fairly shallow as there isn't much water coverage here. The falling tide seems to produce more fish. Light surf rods of around 3.6 m in the 4 to 5 kg class with either a 50 to 60 sized threadline or a 15 cm Alvey reel spooled with 5 to 6 kg line is best when targeting bream, silver trevally and squid. I would suggest using ball sinkers in sizes 000, 00, 0 and 1. The ideal hook sizes for bream and silver trevally would be number 1 to 1/0 circles. You could use a stemmed float (like the ones used when targeting luderick), but I prefer to use a 5 cm bobby cork. The line needs to run freely through the centre of the bobby cork with a stopper at the top.

TACTICS
Best baits are tuna cubes, strips of bonito and mullet for the bream while pilchards and garfish are ideal for tailor and salmon. You could also try floating shallow divers here. You will need to get in a decent cast to get over the boulders though.

BEST TIDE/TIMES
A couple hours either side of the top of the tide would be the preferred time to fish here. If you can coincide this with sunrise or sunset, even better.

AMENITIES
There are no amenities in the immediate area.

KIDS AND FAMILIES
You could bring the kids and family out here, but you will need to make a day of it. The best time would be to fish during the run-in tide as you can cast out onto a sandy bottom and there will be fewer snags.

MIDDLE HEAD

🔍 HOW TO GET THERE

Travel along Middle Head Road, past HMAS Penguin on the left, then right into Chowder Bay Road. You will find a walking track on your left. It is about a sixty minute walk to the rocks at Middle Head. Parking restrictions apply. Gates to the parking areas are locked from 8pm to 6am.

🔍 SNAPSHOT

Platform
HARBOUR/OCEAN ROCKS

Target species
DRUMMER, BREAM, DUSKY FLATHEAD, SAND WHITING, LEATHERJACKET, YELLOWTAIL, SILVER TREVALLY, PAN SIZE SNAPPER, TAILOR, SQUID, AUSTRALIAN SALMON, BONITO, KINGFISH

Best baits
RED & BROWN CRABS, PEELED PRAWNS, BREAD, PINK NIPPERS, HALF PILCHARDS CUNJE, TUNA, MULLET, GREEN WEED, CABBAGE

Best lures
METAL SLICES
POPPERS
SOFT PLASTICS

Best time
EARLY MORNING OR LATE AFTERNOON

SEASONS

Bream **Feb.– May**
Dusky flathead **Nov.– Apr.**
Sand whiting **Oct.– Apr.**
Leatherjacket, yellowtail & squid **Year round**
Pan sized snapper **Winter**
Silver trevally & salmon **Mar.– June**
Tailor, drummer & bonito **Mar.– Aug.**
Luderick **Mar.– Sep.**
Kingfish **Nov.– May**

ABOVE: *Care needs to be taken when walking down the track to Middle Head.*

RIGHT: *Fish as light as possible for bream trevally and drummer.*

Middle Head is a headland situated on the southern side of the entrance to Middle Harbour. It is home to an extensive network of defence fortifications and tunnels, including the Middle Head Fortifications, the Georges Head Battery and the Lower Georges Heights Commanding Position. There are plenty of places to explore, and the forts are quite interesting and historically significant. The track is well-marked and has some information signs. The views of Sydney Harbour are great and it is well worth carrying a picnic lunch to allow more time to enjoy North Head.

TACTICS

I would suggest that you take a couple of buckets with you. One would be for the berley that you will need to use to attract the fish and the other one would be to keep the live yellowtail, mullet and garfish that you can get here. If you are targeting tailor and Australian salmon that pass through here at times, I would suggest that you have a few 30, 40 and 60 g metal lures on hand. You could also try using surface poppers here during the summer months for the odd kingfish or two.

BAITS AND LURES

Red and brown crabs, peeled prawns, bread, pink nippers, half pilchards, cunje, strips of tuna and mullet would be worth a try for bream, trevally, drummer and snapper from here. Green weed and cabbage is the go for drummer and luderick that are caught here during the winter months. Once again berley is an essential item.

BEST TIDE/TIMES

If I was chasing drummer and luderick from here I would prefer to go here when the headland has started to cast a shadow over the water or be there for the first two hours of daylight. It doesn't seem to matter what time of the tide you fish here, as long as it is early in the morning or just before dark. This is a great place to fish when you have a westerly blowing and it has flattened out the swell. Clear, cold and calm water mean the squid will come on the chew.

AMENITIES

There are no amenities here. They are all back at the car park.

KIDS AND FAMILIES

It's not a place to take children, even though you are fishing inside the harbour it is just the same as fishing off the ocean rocks. Make sure that if you do go in here to fish that you check out the swell and sea conditions. This is a spot that can get very dangerous.

ROBERTSON PARK – WATSONS BAY

HOW TO GET THERE

Once you are on Old South Head road travel right to the end, turn right into Roberts Road and then Military Road. Find a parking spot in the nearby car park and walk for about 10 minutes to the water's edge.

ABOVE: *Check out the view looking towards Vaucluse Point.*

RIGHT: *The baths are a good place to cast a line from for bream, whiting and flathead.*

SNAPSHOT

Platform
WHARF
BEACH

Target species
BREAM
DUSKY FLATHEAD
SAND WHITING
LEATHERJACKETS
YELLOWTAIL
SLIMY MACKEREL
SILVER TREVALLY
LUDERICK
SQUID
PAN SIZE SNAPPER
TAILOR
AUSTRALIAN SALMON
KINGFISH
FLOUNDER

Best baits
MULLET, PRAWNS & PILCHARDS.

Best lures
BLADES, SOFT PLASTICS & POPPERS.

Best time
EARLY MORNING

SEASONS
Bream **Feb.– May**
Dusky flathead & Flounder **Nov.– Apr.**
Sand whiting: **Oct.– Apr.**
Leatherjacket, yellowtail & squid **Year round**
Pan sized snapper **Winter**
Silver trevally, Salmon & Slimy Mackerel **Mar.– June**
Tailor **Mar.– Aug.**
Mulloway: **Oct.– May**
Luderick **Mar.– Sept.**
Kingfish **Nov.– May**

You can get here by either driving, catching public transport or the ferry. There are also a number of great restaurants and a pub here to get your lunch or maybe you would prefer to take your own picnic lunch.

TACTICS

I like to throw soft plastics and blades for bream, whiting and flathead here. There have been a number of times when I've been working the shoreline here only to have tailor and salmon chase a school of baitfish close into the shore. This is where those small 40 to 60 g metal lures come in handy. To make it easier, I prefer to carry a small selection of lures in one of the shoulder bags. This means that I can put my box of tricks into the bag along with the fish that I have caught. Blades would have to be one of the most reliable lures here as there is very little to get snagged on.

BAITS AND LURES

Slowly hopped blades work a treat here as do soft plastics rigged on 1/16 oz and 1/12 oz jigheads. When the tailor, kingfish and salmon chase the baitfish you could also try a few surface poppers through the schools.

BEST TIDE/TIMES

The rising tide to the top of the tide seems to push the baitfish into the shore. This will have the surface fish follow them. When the tide starts to fall, the bream, flathead and whiting will lay in wait.

AMENITIES

There are toilets, trees for shade, seats, a small beach, a park and playground here, plus there is a take away restaurant and hotel at the edge of the park.

KIDS AND FAMILIES

Great place to bring the kids. They won't have to cast far to get a nibble and if they get bored you could always shout them a drink or an ice cream. If you don't catch any fish you can always get fish and chips for lunch.

BOTTLE & GLASS ROCKS – VAUCLUSE

HOW TO GET THERE

Once you are on New South Head Road, turn left into Vaucluse Road, which then in turn turns into Wentworth Road. Find a parking spot and walk through Nielsen Park to Vaucluse Point. From here it is just a short walk down to the rocks. Parking restrictions do apply.

SNAPSHOT

Platform
ESTUARY ROCKS AND BEACH.

Target species
BREAM
DUSKY FLATHEAD
SAND WHITING
LEATHERJACKETS
YELLOWTAIL
SILVER TREVALLY
PAN SIZE SNAPPER
TAILOR
SQUID
AUSTRALIAN SALMON
FLOUNDER

Best baits
MULLET
PRAWNS
PILCHARDS

Best lures
METAL SLICES
SOFT PLASTIC
SQUID JIGS

Best time
TOP OF THE TIDE

SEASONS

Bream **February to May**
Dusky flathead & flounder **November to April**
Sand whiting **October to April**
Leatherjacket, yellowtail & squid **Year round**
Pan sized snapper **Winter**
Silver trevally & salmon **March to June**
Tailor **March to August**

ABOVE: *It is a bit of a walk from here to the point, but it is well worth it.*

LEFT: *If the fishing isn't good you could always get a coffee and cake.*

You'll find the idyllic Bottle and Glass Point in the eastern suburbs' renowned Nielsen Park. In this flat, grassy area you'll not only enjoy magnificent views over Vaucluse Bay. There are gorgeous surroundings for a picnic, but fantastic opportunities for fishing, snorkelling, diving and swimming as well. Unload your picnic hamper and watch the sailboats gently bobbing the bay. Listen to the languid sounds of birdsong and water lapping against the rocks, and feel the breeze rustling through the shady trees.

TACTICS

Not a bad place to come and have a fish when the wind is coming in from the south or east as it is fairly protected here. Care will need to be taken when walking along the rocks and you will need to wear some decent footwear. A rod of between 3 to 3.5 m, 4 to 6 kg, a sinker, swivel and a long leader would be ideal when fishing on the north-east corner of this point. If you are going to fish on the north-western side I would suggest that you use a paternoster rig. Try berleying with chopped up pilchards. You will need to throw them out about five metres to get over the kelp found here.

BAITS AND LURES

You could try casting a few soft plastics along the beach here, but don't use them in the enclosed swimming area. Off the rocks you could throw out a few Gulp! Jerkbaits on 1/2 oz jigheads or 70 g metal lures. Surface poppers are worth a shot for tailor, salmon and kingfish that patrol along this set of rocks.

BEST TIDE/TIMES

Fishing at the top of the tide would be the best time to cast a metal or slug type lure or two there. If you are bait fishing I would try early in the morning on a falling tide as the sun will be at your back.

AMENITIES

There are a few BBQs, toilets in Nielsen Park, a picnic area and a meshed swimming enclosure.

KIDS AND FAMILIES

Parking here can be a problem on the weekends and holidays. You will need to arrive fairly early to get a spot. This is a very popular spot for picnickers, walkers and tourists. Great place to take the kids and if they've had enough of fishing they can always play in the park or go for a swim.

CLIFTON GARDENS BATHS

HOW TO GET THERE

Once on Bradleys Head Road, turn left into Thompson Street, right into Burrawong Road, then left into David Street. Find parking and walk for about 10 minutes to the baths in Chowder Bay. Parking restrictions do apply.

SNAPSHOT

Platform
WHARF, ESTUARY ROCKS & BEACH

Target species
BREAM
DUSKY FLATHEAD
SAND WHITING
LEATHERJACKETS
YELLOWTAIL
SILVER TREVALLY
PAN SIZE SNAPPER
TAILOR
SQUID
AUSTRALIAN SALMON
KINGFISH
FLOUNDER

Best baits
PRAWNS, PILCHARDS, SQUID, YELLOWTAIL & MULLET.

Best lures
METAL SLICES, SOFT PLASTICS & BLADES.

Best time
ALL DAY OR NIGHT.

ABOVE: *A very popular landbased spot. Get there early!*

LEFT: *To get the best results, berley with bread.*

One of the loveliest harbour beaches, a long slim stretch of sand with a lengthy jetty, a swimming enclosure, a playground and a large reserve behind. From the beach there are wonderful views over to Neilsen Park and the eastern suburbs, as well as the constant buzz of the harbour with the Manly ferries ploughing by. Rocky bush-covered headlands enclose each end of the beach with bush behind, so the birdlife is plentiful and one feels far away from the big smoke.

TACTICS

During the summer months you will need to get here early to get a spot off the baths. Try using a sinker, swivel and a long leader to cast out wide for bream, flathead and whiting. In close to the baths you can use the paternoster rig with small pieces of peeled prawns for leatherjacket, yellowtail, mullet and slimy mackerel. This is also a great place to catch squid and then use them for live bait to try catching a few bonito, kingfish, tailor and Australian salmon. If the baths do get too crowded you can always walk around the rocks on the western side of the bay and fish into the deep water that is found off the point.

BAITS AND LURES

Blades hopped slowly over the sandy bottom should produce a few flathead, bream and sand whiting. You could also try flicking around a few soft plastics on 1/16 to 1/12 oz jigheads. When the tailor, kingfish and salmon come in here chasing the baitfish you could also try with a few surface poppers, whole pilchards and garfish on a set of ganged hooks through the schools.

BEST TIDE/TIMES

The last 2.5 hours of the rising tide and the first 2 hours of the falling tide for when fishing off the baths. If you're fishing the rocks on the western side of the bay, the run-out tide would be better.

AMENITIES

This stunning park is a popular summertime picnic area for families, with its large grassy area, BBQs, netted swimming pool and a brand new enclosed and sheltered children's playground. There are also toilets, showers and change rooms found here.

KIDS AND FAMILIES

The large and flat reserve has lots of lovely trees, picnic tables, an excellent playground and space for games, bikes and general zooming around. The car park is at one side of the reserve and there is no other road so this is a very safe place for kids.

SEASONS

Bream **Feb.– May**
Dusky flathead & flounder **Nov.– Apr.**
Sand whiting **Oct.– Apr.**
Leatherjacket, yellowtail & squid **Year round**
Pan sized snapper **Winter**
Silver trevally, salmon & slimy mackerel **Mar.– June**
Tailor & bonito **Mar.– Aug.**
Kingfish **Nov.– May**

BRADLEYS HEAD

HOW TO GET THERE

Head south on Bradleys Head Road and travel through the Sydney Harbour National Park. Find parking and it is just a short walk down to the shoreline at the base of Bradleys Head.

SNAPSHOT

Platform
ESTUARY ROCKS & BREAKWALL WITH SANDSTONE WALKWAY.

Target species
BREAM
DUSKY FLATHEAD
SAND WHITING
LEATHERJACKETS
YELLOWTAIL
SILVER TREVALLY
PAN SIZE SNAPPER
TAILOR
MULLOWAY
SQUID
AUSTRALIAN SALMON
KINGFISH
FLOUNDER

Best baits
GARFISH, PILCHARDS, TUNA, MULLET & BONITO.

Best lures
METAL SLICES & SOFT PLASTICS.

Best time
ALL DAY

SEASONS
Bream **Feb.– May**
Dusky flathead & flounder **Nov.–Apr.**
Sand whiting **Oc.–Apr.**
Leatherjacket, yellowtail & squid **Year round**
Pan sized snapper **Winter**
Silver trevally & salmon **March to June**
Tailor & bonito **Mar.–Aug.**
Mulloway **Oct.– May**
Luderick **Mar.– Sep.**
Kingfish **Nov.– May**

ABOVE: *Best fished in a north east wind.*

Bradleys Head is a headland protruding from the north shore of Sydney Harbour, within the metropolitan area of Sydney, New South Wales, Australia. It is named after William Bradley. The foremast of the cruiser HMAS *Sydney*, renowned for taking part in the Royal Australian Navy's first ship against ship engagement in World War I, is mounted on the headland as a memorial to that battle. In June 2000 the mast was rededicated as a monument to all Australian ships and sailors lost in conflict.

TACTICS

Employ light surf rods of around 3.6 m in the 4 to 5 kg class with either a 50 to 60 sized threadline reel or a 15 cm Alvey reel spooled with 5 to 6 kg line for when targeting bream, silver trevally, luderick and squid. When it comes to tailor, salmon and kingfish I would suggest that you use at least a 3.6 m rod in the 6 to 8 kg class with 7 to 10 kg line.

BAITS AND LURES

Whole pilchards and garfish rigged on a set of ganged hooks for tailor, salmon, bonito and kingfish that patrol past here. You could also try using half

pillies, strips of tuna, bonito and mullet for bream, flathead and pan sized snapper. Don't forget to take a few metal slices and slugs for casting out off the rocks for tailor and salmon. Soft plastics rigged on 1/4 to 3/8 oz jigheads can be worked through the sandy patches found here.

BEST TIDE/TIMES

It doesn't seem to matter whether it is the run-in or run-out tide as long as it is near the top of the tide. It can get very snaggy here during the low tides. The main thing to remember here is that you are fishing into very deep water and anything can take your bait.

AMENITIES

Opening hours are from 6am to 8pm each day. There are picnic tables, toilets, a lookout and car park that will not take vehicles longer than 5.3 metres.

KIDS AND FAMILIES

Great facilities in the reserve for the family and kids. Can be a bit of a nightmare for small kids when casting off the rocks here as there are plenty of snags.

LYNE PARK – ROSE BAY

HOW TO GET THERE

Once on New South Head Road at Point Piper travel east to find Lyne Park on the left and the Royal Sydney Golf course on right. Either park in the street or the car park. It is just a 10 minute walk back to the breakwall at the end of Rose Bay. Parking restrictions do apply.

SNAPSHOT

Platform
WHARF, BREAK WALL

Target species
BREAM
DUSKY FLATHEAD
SAND WHITING
LEATHERJACKETS
YELLOWTAIL
SILVER TREVALLY
PAN SIZE SNAPPER
TAILOR
AUSTRALIAN SALMON
SQUID
KINGFISH
FLOUNDER

Best baits
GARFISH, PILCHARDS, TUNA, MULLET & BONITO

Best lures
BLADES, METAL SLICES & SOFT PLASTICS

Best time
HIGH & FALLING TIDE

SEASONS
Bream **Feb.– May**
Dusky flathead & flounder **Nov.– Apr.**
Sand whiting **Oct.– Apr.**
Leatherjacket, yellowtail & squid **Year round**
Pan sized snapper **Winter**
Silver trevally & salmon **Mar.– June**
Tailor **Mar.– Aug.**
Kingfish **Nov.– May**

Bream, luderick, flathead and squid are caught here

Situated across from the Rose Bay ferry, Lynne Park is really easy to find. It has everything you need in a park with a stunning harbour view, pathways by the ocean, a place to kick around a ball or to grab a cold drink. Dogs are welcome and kids will be entertained by the fun and amusement of the protected playground. If you are going to fish from the ferry wharf you will need to take care as there are plenty of boats that come and go from here.

TACTICS

The man-made wall that is situated on the western side of the boat ramp is a great place to target squid at night. Try casting a squid jig out as far as you can before letting them sink to the bottom. Once it has hit the bottom you can either wind the jig in very slowly or you can slowly lift your rod tip and then allow it to slowly sink back down. Bream, flathead, whiting and silver trevally can be berleyed up here. Try mixing chicken layer pellets and squashed up pilchards together. Make a small ball and then throw

out a few at a time. Repeat this process about every 10 minutes. The fish will come, but remember not to berley too much as you will fill them up.

NOTE – *It's illegal to fish on Ferry Wharves during times when the Ferry runs. Check your local wharf for times when fishing is permitted and check if there are any 'No Fishing' signs in the area.*

BAITS AND LURES

Whole and peeled prawns, half pilchards, strip of mullet, bonito, slimy mackerel, tuna and tailor are worth a shot when bait fishing from the wall. The whiting and bream will go for worms and nippers.

BEST TIDE/TIMES

The top of the tide is the best as it can get very shallow here at the bottom of the tide. On the eastern side of the ferry wharf you will find a set of mud flats. Try walking out here at low tide and fish into the deeper water for bream, flathead and whiting.

AMENITIES

A medium sized fenced and gated park with foam floor, there's a range of equipment suited for older kids and toddlers. Well shaded trees with large canopies. Toilets and BBQs are available. There is also a shop across the road.

KIDS AND FAMILIES

Plenty of area in the park for the kids to run around. They can fish off the wharf, but you will need to take care of the many boats that use this wharf and ramp.

MRS MACQUARIES CHAIR

🔍 HOW TO GET THERE

Once on College Street turn right into the Art Gallery Road. Find parking and then walk for about 10 minutes to the end of the point at Mrs Macquarie's Chair. Parking restrictions do apply.

🔍 SNAPSHOT

Platform
BREAKWALL

Target species
BREAM
DUSKY FLATHEAD
SAND WHITING
LEATHERJACKETS
YELLOWTAIL
SILVER TREVALLY
PAN SIZE SNAPPER
TAILOR
AUSTRALIAN SALMON
MULLOWAY
KINGFISH
FLOUNDER

Best baits
PILCHARD, SQUID,
PRAWNS, MULLET,
TUNA & BONITO

Best lures
METAL SLICES,
SURFACE POPPERS,
LARGE SOFT
PLASTICS & SQUID
JIGS

Best time
RUN-IN TIDE

SEASONS
Bream **Feb.– May**
Dusky flathead &
flounder **Nov.– Apr.**
Sand whiting **Oct.– Apr.**
Leatherjacket, yellowtail
& squid **Year round**
Pan sized snapper
Winter
Silver trevally &
salmon **Mar.– June**
Tailor & bonito
Mar.– Aug.
Mulloway **Oct.– May**
Kingfish **Nov.– May**

It can get very glary on the western side of Mrs Macquarie's Chair in the afternoon. So remember to take that sun cream with you.

Mrs Macquarie's Chair, otherwise known as Lady Macquarie's Chair, provides one of the best vantage points in Sydney. The historic chair was carved out of a rock ledge for Governor Lachlan Macquarie's wife, Elizabeth, as she was known to visit the area. Mrs Macquarie's Point is the best-known picnic spot in Sydney, but for very good reason. It probably has the best view in the city.

TACTICS

Try using a paternoster rig with two hooks. One hook should be laced with a half pillie and the other with e a strip of mullet. I have successfully used a number 6 ball sinker down onto a whole pilchard rigged onto a set of 5/0 ganged hooks for tailor, flathead and the odd mulloway. You could also try using a large bobby cork to suspend your bait about 3 to 4 m below it for tailor, salmon and kingfish. Due to the fact that tailor will come past here with the rising tide I suggest you also take a few metal lures with you. Casting and slowly retrieving a whole pilchard or garfish rigged onto a set of ganged hooks is always worth a shot in the early parts of the morning.

BAITS AND LURES

Whole pilchards and garfish rigged on a set of ganged hooks will take tailor, salmon, bonito and kingfish that patrol past here. You could also try using half pillies, strips of tuna, bonito and mullet for bream, flathead and pan sized snapper. Don't forget to take a few metal slices and slugs for casting out off the rocks for tailor and salmon. Soft plastics rigged on 1/4 to 3/8 oz jigheads can be worked through the sandy patches found here.

BEST TIDE/TIMES

The run-in tide works best here because you will be able to use the current that runs past here to take your bait out onto the sandy bottom.

AMENITIES

The point where Mrs Macquarie's Chair is situated is in the Royal Botanic Gardens. Here you will find seating, covered area for shade, toilets and a café.

KIDS AND FAMILIES

If the kids get bored with fishing you could always take them for a walk through the Royal Botanic Gardens to have a look at the huge eels and carp in the ponds.

PIER 2 & 3

HOW TO GET THERE

Travel north down
Sussex Road until you
reach Hickson Road.

ABOVE: *Anglers fishing off Pier 2 and 3 on the run-out tide.*

LEFT: *Flathead can be caught while fishing off this wharf.*

There are a number of piers in this area, but it seems that Pier 1 attracts many of the shorebased anglers from Sydney. The water depth is around 12 m, so you don't have to cast very far. Rubbish left behind by angler seems to be an issue here so do the responsible thing and take it with you.

TACTICS

Many anglers make the mistake of trying to cast out as far as possible here. Try using a paternoster rig and lower it down to the bottom directly beside the wharf. Yellowtail and mullet can be berleyed up here. Once you catch a few of them try suspending one under a bobby cork. You will find that there are a few places where you can stick the butt of the rod into, but I would suggest that you don't leave the rod un-attended as there are some big fish that patrol this pier.

BAITS AND LURES

Whole pilchards and garfish rigged on a set of ganged hooks for tailor, salmon, bonito and kingfish that patrol past here. You could also try using half pillies, strips of tuna, bonito and mullet for bream, flathead and pan sized snapper. Don't forget to take a few metal slices and slugs for casting out off the rocks for tailor and salmon. Soft plastics rigged on 1/4 to 3/8 oz jigheads can be worked through the sandy patches found here.

BEST TIDE/TIMES

It doesn't seem to matter what tide you fish here, as the water is very deep.

AMENITIES

You will have to walk to the nearest shops to find any. Parking has to be paid for if you are going to park your car close to where you are fishing.

KIDS AND FAMILIES

Great place to take the kids for a fish, but you will need to remember you are on a wharf that is about three metres above the water. Care will need to be taken as there isn't many access points down to the water if they fall in.

SNAPSHOT

Platform
WHARF

Target species
BREAM
DUSKY FLATHEAD
SAND WHITING
LEATHERJACKETS
YELLOWTAIL
SILVER TREVALLY
PAN SIZE SNAPPER
TAILOR
MULLOWAY
AUSTRALIAN SALMON
KINGFISH

Best baits
GARFISH,
PILCHARDS,
MULLET & TUNA

Best lures
METAL LURES,
SQUID JIGS & SOFT PLASTICS

Best time
RUN-IN TIDE

SEASONS

Bream **Feb.– May**
Dusky flathead &
flounder **Nov.– Apr.**
Sand whiting **Oct.– Apr.**
Leatherjacket &
yellowtail **Year round**
Pan sized snapper **Winter**
Silver trevally &
salmon **Mar.– June**
Tailor & bonito **Mar.– Aug.**
Mulloway **Oct.– May**
Kingfish **Nov.– May**

BLUES POINT RESERVE

🔍 HOW TO GET THERE

Once on Miller Street at North Sydney travel south into Blues Point Road. Park at the end of this road and walk about 5 to 10 minutes to the point at the end.

🔍 SNAPSHOT

Platform
RETAINING WALL

Target species
MULLOWAY
BREAM
DUSKY FLATHEAD
SAND WHITING
LEATHERJACKETS
YELLOWTAIL
SILVER TREVALLY
PAN SIZE SNAPPER
TAILOR
LUDERICK
GARFISH
MULLET
AUSTRALIAN SALMON
KINGFISH
FLOUNDER

Best baits
LIVE BAITS, PILCHARD, MULLET, BLOOD WORMS, TUNA & GREEN WEED

Best lures
METAL SLICES, SQUID JIGS, SOFT PLASTICS & POPPERS

Best time
RUN-IN OR RUN-OUT TIDE, EARLY MORNING, LATE AFTERNOON

SEASONS

Bream **Feb.– May**
Dusky flathead & flounder **Nov.– April**
Sand whiting **Oct.– Apr.**
Garfish, leatherjacket, mullet & yellowtail **Year round**
Pan sized snapper: **Winter**
Silver trevally & slimy mackerel **Mar.– June**
Tailor **Mar.– Aug.**
Mulloway **Oct.– May**
Luderick **Mar.– Sep.**
Kingfish **Nov.– May**

ABOVE: *The water is fairly deep off the point. Great place to target bream, flathead, trevally, mulloway and kingfish on the run-out tide.*

LEFT: *This angler didn't own all of these rods. There were a number of anglers fishing off this point.*

Blues Point Reserve is arguably the finest place in Sydney from which to view the harbour, the bridge and the Opera House. For that reason Blues Point Reserve is one of the finest places in Sydney to enjoy a picnic while having a fish. The water here is very deep which makes it very attractive to passing kingfish and mulloway.

TACTICS

Plenty of mulloway, snapper and big dusky flathead have been caught here during the summer months. You will need to get a decent cast in here to get your rig out past the kelp and snags. Try using a number 5 to 6 ball sinker that slides down onto the bait or the paternoster rig. During the autumn to winter months you will be in with a good chance of catching luderick on cabbage or weed. I would suggest you use a mixture of bread, sand and chopped up weed and cabbage for berley. It is also worth having a few squid jigs and metal lures in the bag during the cooler months of the year.

BAITS AND LURES

Whole pilchards or garfish that have been rigged onto a set of 5/0 ganged hooks. Five and 7 inch soft plastics worked slowly along the bottom could get you into a mulloway or two.

BEST TIDE/TIMES

If you are fishing on the eastern side of Blues Point I would suggest that you fish the run-out tide in the afternoon and if you are going to fish the run-in tide you would be better off going to western side of the point in the morning. This will allow you to use the current, along with your casting ability to get the rig out onto a sandy patch, while not having the sun directly shining onto your face.

AMENITIES

There are toilets and shops nearby. Near to where you can park is a small sandy beach that you could have a picnic on, or maybe you would prefer to use the grassed area.

KIDS AND FAMILIES

Parking here at times can be a real problem. You will need to get here earlier to get a parking spot as there are only a few close to this spot.

HOW TO GET THERE 🔍

At Greenwich Road turn off Princess Highway, left at Manns Avenue, left into George Street, right at Victoria Street and then left at Prospect Street. Park and walk about 5–10 minutes to Manns Point Park. Parking restrictions do apply.

ABOVE: *This is another one of those deep water spots in the harbour to target a mulloway or two.*

RIGHT: *As you can see from the picture taken at low tide, there are plenty of oysters on the rock, which will in-turn attract bream at high tide.*

Mann's Point has a small, but narrow boat ramp with limited parking. There is no beaching area or proper jetty, unless you're ready to climb over a fence, or take a trip around the corner. This is a great place for the landbased angler to come in the late afternoon, to try for a number of species. Not the best place to fish in a southerly breeze as the wind will be right in your face. The wall along the rocky foreshore has plenty of room to lay out a few rods against the chain wire fence.

TACTICS

This is a place where you will need to be able to cast out a fair way so that you can get away from the snags at your feet. Although you could try fishing for leatherjacket at your feet with a paternoster rig baited with small pieces of prawn or squid. Tailor and salmon sometimes come in in here to chase baitfish so it's worth having metal slices on hand. You could also try working a few soft plastics and blades out wide for flathead, pan sized snapper, silver trevally, bream and the odd mulloway. Try catching a couple of yellowtail or mullet that you

can berley up here and use them for live bait for mulloway, flathead and kingfish.

BAITS AND LURES

Whole pilchards, garfish, yellowtail, slimy mackerel and mullet would be the best for mulloway and kingfish. Strips of tuna, mullet, slimy mackerel, yellowtail and half pilchards would be the go for bream, trevally and flathead.

BEST TIDE/TIMES

The time of the tide doesn't seem to matter here, but the direction of the wind does. Not the best place to fish at when the wind is coming from the south. Better fished during a northerly wind.

AMENITIES

There are no amenities here, but there is parking for about 30 cars. There is a small park that the kids can play in if they get sick of fishing.

KIDS AND FAMILIES

There is a walking trail from the upper to lower level where you will find picnic benches and seats. This is also the base for Greenwich Sailing Club.

SNAPSHOT 🔍

Platform
ESTUARY ROCKS, ELEVATED GRASSED AREA

Target species
BREAM
DUSKY FLATHEAD
SAND WHITING
LEATHERJACKETS
YELLOWTAIL
SILVER TREVALLY
PAN SIZE SNAPPER
TAILOR
AUSTRALIAN SALMON
MULLET, GARFISH
KINGFISH, FLOUNDER

Best baits
PILCHARDS, GARFISH, SLIMY MACKEREL, YELLOWTAIL, PRAWNS

Best lures
METAL SLICES, & LARGE SOFT PLASTICS

Best time
ANY TIME OTHER THAN IN A SOUTHERLY WIND

SEASONS
Bream **Feb.– May**
Dusky flathead & flounder **Nov.– April**
Sand whiting **Oct.– Apr.**
Garfish, leatherjacket, mullet & yellowtail **Year round**
Pan sized snapper: **Winter**
Silver trevally & salmon **Mar.– June**
Tailor **Mar.– Aug.**
Mulloway **Oct.– May**
Luderick **Mar.– Sep.**
Kingfish **Nov.– May**

CLARKES POINT

HOW TO GET THERE

On Woolwich Road at Hunters Hill, travel east and turn right into Egin Street then into Clarke Place. Walk through Clarkes Point Reserve to the breakwall at the water's edge. Parking restrictions apply.

SNAPSHOT

Platform
GRASSED AREA, ELEVATED ROCKWALL

Target species
BREAM,
DUSKY FLATHEAD,
SAND WHITING,
LEATHERJACKETS,
YELLOWTAIL,
SILVER TREVALLY,
PAN SIZE SNAPPER,
TAILOR,
AUSTRALIAN SALMON,
MULLET, GARFISH
KINGFISH, MULLOWAY

Best baits
PILCHARD, GARFISH,
LIVE BAIT, MULLET,
SQUID, GREEN WEED,
PRAWNS

Best lures
METAL SLICES,
SURFACE POPPERS,
BLADES, HEAVILY
WEIGHTED SOFT
PLASTICS

Best time
RUN-OUT TIDE, DAY
OR NIGHT

SEASONS

Bream **Feb.– May**
Dusky flathead & flounder **Nov.– April**
Sand whiting **Oct.– Apr.**
Garfish, leatherjacket, mullet & yellowtail **Year round**
Pan sized snapper: **Winter**
Silver trevally & salmon **Mar.– June**
Tailor **Mar.– Aug.**
Mulloway **Oct.– May**
Luderick **Mar.– Sep.**
Kingfish **Nov.– May**

ABOVE: *Try working squid jigs from the shore here on a run-out tide during the afternoon.*

RIGHT: *This angler is very prepared with his landing net, luderick outfit, esky and trolley.*

At the far end of the leafy French settlement of Hunters Hill lies Woolwich Peninsula. The Woolwich peninsula consists of a succession of knolls leading down to the meeting point of the Parramatta and Lane Cove Rivers. Weathering has resulted in a spur off the Woolwich ridgeline forming Clarkes Point at the meeting of the two rivers. The reserve is a popular weekend spot for picnickers and anglers alike. If you need a change from fishing you could always go for a walk in Kelly Bush Reserve.

TACTICS

Fish in close with a stemmed float for luderick. You need to berley to keep them around your float. You will need to find either green weed or cabbage elsewhere and bring it in with you as there is very little on the rocks here. Also, due to the fact that the wall is a fair bit off the water you will need to bring a long handled landing net with you. Once you have caught a fish you can keep them fresh by putting them into a bucket or hang a keeper net over the side of the wall. Just keep an eye out for rats that will take a liking to your fish.

BAITS AND LURES

Surface poppers and large soft plastics can be worked here either early in the morning or just before the sun sets. When there has been a lot of fresh in the water from a flood you could try using floating deep divers for a mulloway or two. Half and one ounce blades can be hopped over the bottom here, but you will need to judge it right when you make the last lift as you can easily get snagged up close into the rocks.

BEST TIDE/TIMES

You will find that the eastern side of this point is fished the most. Therefore the run-out tide would be the best time to fish from here as your baits and rigs will stay away from the snags that are in close. During the cooler months of the year the luderick will school up here and quite often it can be shoulder-to-shoulder fishing when they're on the chew.

AMENITIES

There are plenty of toilets on the reserve and barbeques.

KIDS AND FAMILIES

The reserve is a popular Sunday picnic destination as it has barbeque and other facilities. It also has one of the more extensive grassy slopes on Sydney Harbour and is popular for fishing or just to lie down and watch the boats and yachts as they go by.

ELKINGTON PARK – BALMAIN

HOW TO GET THERE 🔍

From Darling Road at Rozelle turn left into Young Street. Proceed down to the T section; straight ahead you will see Elkington Park. Find a parking spot and walk through the park to the water's edge until you come to White Horse Point.

There is a park on top of this point, but the fishing is best from the rock below.

LEFT: Remember to let the two, three and four inch Gulp Shrimps to stay on the bottom for a few seconds before jerking them off the bottom.

This park juts out on a rocky Balmain Peninsula, looking out to the Parramatta River and Cockatoo Island. It has the well-manicured but rambling feel of an old English estate – picturesque, pretend wilderness. A lovely spot close to the water and great to visit any time of the day. There are tall palm trees and wide, heavy figs with plenty of shade, and a bit of a hill to climb when you're walking back home. It is about a minute walk down to Dawn Fraser Pool. Best of all, if you go right to the end of the peninsula, you can explore rocky sandstone caves and alcoves. The end of the peninsula is also an off-leash dog area, so long as you don't get too close to the kids' play equipment.

TACTICS

The lights at this place will attract squid at night, so make sure you have a few jigs handy. Try using 2.5 to 3.5 weighted jigs for the best results. The shoreline here fishes well for leatherjacket, whiting, dusky flathead and bream. Work the baits and lures close as possible to the edge. This is a great place to use two rods at the same time. Try casting parallel to the shoreline and bounce floating shallow diving lures over the rocks and through the kelp, while at the same time having another rod set up with a half pillie or peeled prawn on it. The rig I would be using would be a sinker down onto the swivel with a leader of about 1 to 1.5 m long.

BAITS AND LURES

Pilchard, whitebait, frog mouthed pilchards, strips of squid, whole prawns and strips of mullet, tuna and slimy mackerel are worth a shot. Soft plastics can be worked in an umbrella fashion from the shoreline. A cast of about 20 m would do the job.

BEST TIDE/TIMES

The rising tide to the top of the tide seems to push the baitfish into the shore. This will have the surface fish follow them. When the tide starts to fall, the bream, flathead and whiting will lay in wait. The odd mulloway can be lured up here during the slower parts of the tide. Just remember to work them very slowly

AMENITIES

Free street parking is available, and toilets are located on-site. The park has a covered rotunda that can be used as sun or rain protection for the family.

KIDS AND FAMILIES

Enclosed play equipment for toddlers and older children is available here. The area also boasts a fairly basic small playground area with swings and an enclosed area with slippery dip, mini-rock climbing, walking bridge, and monkey bars. There are no shade sails over the playground, but plenty of big old trees for protection, and the Jacaranda trees, when in bloom, are absolutely divine. Plenty of grassy area to run around on and a path for scooters.

SNAPSHOT 🔍

Platform
GRASSED AREA, ELEVATED ROCK WALL

Target species
BREAM
DUSKY FLATHEAD
SAND WHITING
LEATHERJACKETS
YELLOWTAIL
SILVER TREVALLY
PAN SIZE SNAPPER
TAILOR
MULLET
GARFISH
AUSTRALIAN SALMON
FLOUNDER

Best baits
PILCHARDS, GARFISH, PRAWNS, MULLET

Best lures
SOFT PLASTICS, BLADES

Best time
HIGH TIDE

SEASONS

Bream **Feb.– May**
Dusky flathead & flounder **Nov.– Apr.**
Sand whiting **Oct.– April**
Garfish, leatherjacket, mullet, yellowtail, squid **Year round**
Pan sized snapper **Winter**
Silver trevally, & salmon **Mar.– June**
Tailor **Mar.– Aug.**

GLADESVILLE BRIDGE EAST

🔍 HOW TO GET THERE

From Victoria Road at Huntleys Cove you will need to turn right at the set of lights at Huntleys Point Road. It is about 2 to 3 minutes from here to Betts Park. Then it is a short walk to the pylons of the Gladesville Bridge.

🔍 SNAPSHOT

Platform
ROCKWALL

Target species
BREAM
DUSKY FLATHEAD
SAND WHITING
LEATHERJACKETS
YELLOWTAIL
SILVER TREVALLY
PAN SIZE SNAPPER
TAILOR
MULLOWAY
FLOUNDER

Best baits
LIVE BAIT, MULLET, SLIMY MACKEREL, PINK NIPPER, BLOOD WORMS, PRAWNS

Best lures
LARGE SOFT PLASTICS, DEEP DIVING LURES

Best time
LOW LIGHT PERIODS
– HIGH OR LOW TIDE

SEASONS

Bream **Feb.– May**
Dusky flathead **Nov.– April**
Sand whiting **Oct.– April**
Leatherjacket **Year round**
Yellowtail **Year round**
Pan sized snapper **Winter**
Silver trevally **Mar.– May**
Flounder **Nov.– April**
Tailor **Mar.– Aug.**
Mulloway **Oct.– May**

The deep water on the western side of the Gladesville Bridge is easily accessed.

BELOW: Work those blades in the deep water at the base of the bridge.

Gladesville Bridge is an arch bridge near Gladesville that spans the Parramatta River. It links the suburbs of Huntley's Point and Drummoyne and it is a few kilometers upstream of the more famous Sydney Harbour Bridge. At the time of its completion in 1964, Gladesville Bridge was the longest single span concrete arch ever constructed. There is easy access to either side of the base of this bridge and the eastern side has the deeper water.

TACTICS

Gladesville Bridge can be quite a productive spot for mulloway. If you try the north-western corner opposite the marina you will see a small cluster of rocks. It's off these rocks that there is a drop off of around 15 to 20 m; a good spot to try on a run-in tide. It's also reputed that the Gladesville Wharf fish's quite well for leatherjacket on early mornings. Cast out into and around the moored boats from the eastern side of the bridge around the moorings on the hunters hill side for bream, big flathead and lesser kingfish.

BAITS AND LURES

You can catch your own live yellowtail and squid here, but you will need to work hard at it. Whole dead fish like yellowtail, slimy mackerel, mullet and garfish will also attract a mulloway or two while fishing here. Strips of squid, tuna, mullet and bonito make for great bait for trevally, bream and flathead that can be caught here on the rising tide.

BEST TIDE/TIMES

Arguably the best place in Sydney to catch the elusive jewfish. I have caught many a mulloway here and so have many other anglers. I have found the best time to go and chase them is after the last ferry.

AMENITIES

On the eastern side of the bridge there is a small marina where you can get a drink or maybe a coffee.

KIDS AND FAMILIES

This spot is a bit hard to fish from if you are a small kid, but if you can get a decent cast out, you will be in with a chance of hooking up to a bream or flathead.

BLACKWALL POINT – HOWLEY PARK

HOW TO GET THERE

Once on Great North Road at Five Dock, travel along and turn right at the roundabout at Blackwall Point Road. From here it is about a two kilometre dive to Blackwall Point Reserve in Bortfield Drive.

ABOVE: *The water out from here is very deep. Worth a shot for mulloway at either the top or bottom of the tide.*

RIGHT: *Don't be put off from using big soft plastics for dusky flathead. This 45cm flathead scoffed down a 4 inch Gulp Shrimp.*

SNAPSHOT

Platform
RETAINING WALL

Target species
BREAM
DUSKY FLATHEAD
SAND WHITING
LEATHERJACKETS
YELLOWTAIL
SILVER TREVALLY
PAN SIZE SNAPPER
TAILOR
AUSTRALIAN SALMON
KINGFISH
FLOUNDER
MULLOWAY

Best baits
PINK NIPPERS,
BLOOD WORMS,
SQUID

Best lures
SOFT PLASTICS

Best time
HIGH TIDE

SEASONS

Bream **Feb.– May**
Dusky flathead **Nov.– April**
Sand whiting **Oct.– April**
Leatherjacket **Year round**
Yellowtail **Year round**
Pan sized snapper **Winter**
Silver trevally **Mar.– June**
Flounder **Nov.– April**
Salmon **Mar.–June**
Tailor **Mar.– Aug.**
Mulloway **Oct.– May**
Kingfish **Nov.– May**

Originally there were five sandstone crevices along the shoreline, which were thought to resemble small docks. Two of the 'docks' were covered by the foundations of the first Gladesville Bridge. The water drops away very quickly here and there can be a fair amount of tide pushing past this point at times. Care will need to be taken when fishing here, as the rocks can at times be very slippery and loose. Good footwear is a must when fishing here.

TACTICS

This stretch of shoreline has very deep water close in, so you don't have to cast out too far to get to the passing fish. A rod length of somewhere between 3 to 3.5 m in length and 4 to 8 kg breaking strain will do the job of getting a good cast in and lifting the fish out of the water. Spool your reels up with at least six kilogram line. I would use either the paternoster rig or a sinker down onto the swivel with a fluorocarbon leader of 1 to 1.5 m in length.

BAITS AND LURES

Squid, pilchard, prawn, mullet gut, whitebait and frog mouth pilchards are all worth a shot. You could also try using blood, tube and beach worms for some of the monster whiting that live here.

BEST TIDE/TIMES

It doesn't seem to matter which part of the tide you fish here. I would concentrate my times to either early mornings or later in the afternoon.

AMENITIES

There is a bit of a park, but not much else here for the kids.

KIDS AND FAMILIES

This spot is a bit hard to fish from if you are a small kid, but if you can get a decent cast out, you will be in with a chance of hooking up to a bream or flathead. There are not many places for them to put their rods down. They will need to hold onto them.

FIVE DOCK BAY

🔍 HOW TO GET THERE

On Lyons Road at Five Dock travel towards the suburb of Drummoyne, and turn left at Bayswater Road. From here it is about one kilometre to Talpin Park. There is plenty of off street parking with a five minute walk to the sandstone retaining wal on this side of Five Dock Bay.

🔍 SNAPSHOT

Platform
BREAKWALL

Target species
BREAM
DUSKY FLATHEAD
SAND WHITING
LEATHERJACKETS
YELLOWTAIL
SILVER TREVALLY
PAN SIZE SNAPPER
TAILOR
AUSTRALIAN SALMON
MULLET
GARFISH
FLOUNDER
MULLOWAY

Best baits
BLOOD WORMS, PINK NIPPER, PRAWNS

Best lures
SOFT PLASTICS, DIVING HARDBODIES, BLADES

Best time
EARLY MORNING AND HIGH TIDE

SEASONS

Bream **Feb.– May**
Dusky flathead & flounder **Nov.– April**
Sand whiting **Oct.– April**
Garfish, leatherjacket, mullet & yellowtail **Year round**
Yellowtail **Year round**
Pan sized snapper **Winter**
Silver trevally & salmon **Mar.– June**
Tailor **Mar.– Aug.**
Mulloway **Oct.– May**

Great place to bring the kids as you don't have to cast far for a chance of a fish.

There is a concrete path that goes around at least half of Five Dock Bay. It is from here that you can either bait or lure fish. What you have to remember is that it is a very popular walking area, so you will need to keep an eye out for people walking by behind you when you are casting. The water here is not that deep, only about 3 to 4 m at the most.

TACTICS

A cast of about 15 to 20 m will get you out past most of the snags in this bay. This is approximately where the water depth will increase to 3 to 4 metres. Try using a sinker down onto the swivel with a one metre leader. You could also rig up a number 3 or 3 ball sinker down onto the bait and cast this out as well. You will need to keep an eye out for push bike riders, joggers and walkers. You don't want to hook one with your back cast. This would be one of the few places that I wouldn't berley – the main reason being that I couldn't throw it out far enough to be effective.

BAITS AND LURES

Live baits like blood worms, pink nippers, poddy mullet, garfish and yellowtail would have to be the prime baits for when fishing from the shoreline. Just up the road at Drummoyne Bait and Tackle you can get a few of these live baits.

BEST TIDE/TIMES

As this is a fairly shallow bay, the best time to fish from shore would be during the run-up tide. You could also fish the first hour of the run-out tide. The wind can swirl around in this bay, so I would check out the strength of the wind before coming here to fish. A light breeze would be the best.

AMENITIES

There is a park at the rear of the boat ramp that has a playground and toilets. Further around in the bay there are a couple of playing fields.

KIDS AND FAMILIES

There is a walking track around this bay, plus a couple of playing fields.

ABOVE: *There are plenty of spots to fish from, at Peacock Point.*

RIGHT: *This 18 cm whiting was thrown up by this 84 cm dusky.*

SNAPSHOT

Platform
RETAINING WALL

Target species
BREAM
DUSKY FLATHEAD
SAND WHITING
LEATHERJACKETS
YELLOWTAIL
SILVER TREVALLY
PAN SIZE SNAPPER
TAILOR
AUSTRALIAN
SALMON
FLOUNDER
MULLOWAT

Best baits
BLOOD WORMS,
PINK NIPPER,
PRAWNS.

Best lures
SOFT PLASTICS,
DIVING
HARDBODIES AND
BLADES

Best time
EARLY MORNING
AND HIGH TIDE

SEASONS
Bream **Feb.– May**
Dusky flathead &
flounder **Nov.– April**
Sand whiting **Oct.– April**
Leatherjacket & yellowtail
Year round
Pan sized snapper **Winter**
Silver trevally & salmon
Mar.– June
Tailor **Mar.– Aug.**
Mulloway **Oct.– May**

One thing that stands out at Peacock Point is the old boat anchor. From here, if you look to the opposite side of the bay you will be able to see wharfs on Jones Bay at Pyrmont and Johnstons Bay towards Anzac Bridge.

TACTICS

There will be a fair amount of boat traffic past this point time during the day. It is best fished in the early parts of the morning, late afternoons or during the night. I would suggest that you take a long handled net, as you are about 3 to 4 m above the shore. Try using the paternoster rig as this will keep your baits off the bottom and away from most of the snags. When you get there you will see that there is a fair amount of kelp up against the shoreline. It is this kelp that the leatherjacket will live and feed in.

BAITS AND LURES

This is a great place to spin for tailor and kingfish on a rising tide with poppers and large metal lures. You could also try casting out a few floating deep diving hardbodies and slowly rolling them back

BEST TIDE/TIMES

The run-in tide seems to produce more fish, but don't let this stop you from fishing the run-out tide. Try to coincide them during the low-light periods of the day.

AMENITIES

There aren't any.

KIDS AND FAMILIES

You can bring the kids here, but remember you will need to be able to cast out for them if they can't get the required distance.

BICENTENNIAL PARK – ANNADALE

HOW TO GET THERE

Once on Parramatta Road at Annandale, travelling towards the city, turn left at the set of lights at Johnston Street. Travel north until you come to a set of lights at The Crescent. Cross The Crescent into Chaplam where you can park. It is only a short walk through the park to the retaining walls at the end.

SNAPSHOT

Platform
RETAINING WALL.

Target species
BREAM
DUSKY FLATHEAD
SAND WHITING
LEATHERJACKETS
YELLOWTAIL
SILVER TREVALLY
PAN SIZE SNAPPER
TAILOR
AUSTRALIAN SALMON
FLOUNDER

Best baits
BLOOD WORMS,
PINK NIPPER,
PRAWNS

Best lures
SOFT PLASTICS,
DIVING HARDBODIES,
BLADES

Best time
EARLY MORNING AND
HIGH TIDE

SEASONS

Bream **Feb.– May**
Dusky flathead
Nov.– April
Sand whiting
Oct.– April
Leatherjacket
Year round
Yellowtail **Year round**
Flounder **Nov.– Apr.**
Mullet **Year round**

ABOVE: *This gentleman was targeting mullet to use later as bait.*

RIGHT: *Low tide will reveal a lot of hidden treasures for the observant angler.*

Bicentennial Park is a large area of parkland located 16 km west of the Sydney central business district in the local government area of Auburn Council. Bicentennial Park is a 40 ha natural heritage site featuring an important wetland ecosystem and parklands. It offers visitors recreation, nature-based tours, environmental education and outdoor event experiences. The park has picnic areas, playgrounds, pathways and cycle ways, access to the wetlands, salt marsh and bird hides.

TACTICS

I would take a couple of rods to fish here. One would be rigged with a small ball sinker straight down onto the hook and the other outfit would be rigged up to use either a small floating hard bodied lure or a lightly weighted soft plastics. The bottom here is made up mainly of mud, so I would be venturing into the water to retrieve that snagged lure. For a bit of extra distance you could try casting out and retrieving a small bladed lure.

BAITS AND LURES

Blood worms, pink nippers and the like would get eaten very quickly here by small baitfish. I prefer to use either salted down pilchards, mullet and slimy mackerel strips. You could also try cubing a few pieces of tuna.

BEST TIDE/TIMES

As the water is fairly shallow here I would concentrate my fishing time to about an hour and a half either side of the top of the tide.

AMENITIES

There is a fenced playground with nearby toilets and the area is suitable for toddlers. There are sun shades, tables, a BBQ, car parking and nearby is a bike path.

KIDS AND FAMILIES

This large playground is hidden away between Annandale and Blackwattle Bay. The equipment is fantastic and there is so much here for all ages that a visit can last for hours.

HENLEY

HOW TO GET THERE 🔍

Once on Victoria Road at Gladesville, travel towards the Gladesville Bridge, turn right at the lights at Crown Street, then right at Sherwin Street, then left into Dick Street.

ABOVE: *There are a couple of rod holders concreted into the rocks here. Tide does rip past here at times.*

RIGHT: *You will need to up size those leaders when fishing here with blades as the bottom is fairly snaggy.*

SNAPSHOT 🔍

Platform
RETAINING WALL

Target species
BREAM
DUSKY FLATHEAD
SAND WHITING
LEATHERJACKETS
YELLOWTAIL
SILVER TREVALLY
PAN SIZE SNAPPER
TAILOR
AUSTRALIAN SALMON
FLOUNDER

Best baits
BLOOD WORMS, PINK NIPPER, PRAWNS

Best lures
SOFT PLASTICS, DIVING HARDBODIES, BLADES

Best time
EARLY MORNING AND HIGH TIDE

Travel along Victoria Road towards the city of Sydney and turn right at a set of lights at Crown Street. Then turn right at Sherwin Street and then left into Dick Street. Once you get to the end of this street you can take a short walk to a small grassed area at the end of the road to a place called Three Brothers Rock.

TACTICS

I would suggest that you break out the 3 to 3.5 m rods, spool them up with 6 kg line and bring them down to this spot. The tide does move around here at times very quickly, so I would suggest that you use either a 1/4 oz to 1/2 oz star or snapper sinker on a paternoster rig. This ensures the sinker keeps on the bottom, while allowing the baited two hook rig to move with the current. You could also try rigging up an outfit with large paddle tail soft plastics and casting up current. This will allow you to work them slowly back down with the current. Much the same as you would work them on a breakwall.

BAITS AND LURES

You can tend to get a lot of small fish here so I would suggest that you try using salted pilchards, tuna, slimy mackerel and mullet. Fresh squid, octopus and fillets of yellowtail would also be worth a try.

BEST TIDE/TIMES

It doesn't seem to matter at what part of the tide you fish here, but if there is a strong southerly wind blowing you will need to find somewhere else to go as it will be blowing directly into your face.

AMENITIES

The nearest toilet would be at the closest petrol station.

KIDS AND FAMILIES

Not a lot to do here for the kids. That is unless they want to have a fish.

SEASONS

Bream **Feb.– May**
Dusky flathead
Nov.– April
Sand whiting
Oct.– April
Leatherjacket
Year round
Yellowtail **Year round**
Flounder **Nov.– Apr.**
Mullet **Year round**

BEDLAM POINT

HOW TO GET THERE

Once on Victoria Road at Gladesville you will need to veer off to the right into Punt Road. Upon arriving you will come across a small amount of off street parking and it is just a short walk down to Bedlam Bay Park.

SNAPSHOT

Platform
ESTUARY ROCKS.

Target species
BREAM
DUSKY FLATHEAD
SAND WHITING
LEATHERJACKETS
YELLOWTAIL
SILVER TREVALLY
PAN SIZE SNAPPER
TAILOR
FLOUNDER
MULLOWAY

Best baits
PRAWNS, PINK NIPPERS, BLOOD WORMS

Best lure
HARDBODIED DEEP DIVERS

Best time
ALL DAY

ABOVE: *If a southerly wind is blowing and you can't fish Bedlam Point try going around the corner to the wharf at Banjo Peterson Park.*

RIGHT: *Fishing light with either strips of squid or peeled prawns could have you tangling with these fish species.*

SEASONS

Bream **Feb.– May**
Dusky flathead
Nov.– Apr.
Sand whiting **Oct.– Apr.**
Leatherjacket **Year round**
Yellowtail **Year round**
Pan sized snapper
Winter
Silver trevally
Mar.– June
Flounder **Nov.– Apr.**
Tailor **Mar– Aug.**
Mulloway **Oct.– May**

There is a walk by the Parramatta River, bounded by the Great North Road and the Old Gladesville Hospital, encompassing significant artifacts including remains of old hospital gardens, a stone ferry wharf and Aboriginal sites. The walk includes steep and complex terrain in bushland, as well as open park-like space down to the water's edge.

TACTICS

The fishing here is very similar to that of the previous location (Nelson). And as such the same tactics can be implemented.

BAITS AND LURES

Squid, pilchards, prawns, mullet gut and strips, whitebait and frog mouth pilchards would be worth a shot. You could also try using blood, tube and beach worms for some of the monster whiting that live here.

BEST TIDE/TIMES

It doesn't seem to matter at what part of the tide you fish here, but if there is a strong southerly wind blowing you will need to find somewhere else to go as it will be blowing directly into your face.

AMENITIES

New elements including an amenities building, interpretive signage, bridges, steps and viewing platforms are carefully woven into the landscape to preserve view corridors and to avoid damage to cultural sites.

KIDS AND FAMILIES

There is a small area for them to run around, but this is mainly a fishing spot.

PRINCE EDWARD PARK

HOW TO GET THERE

Once on Parramatta Road heading towards the city you need to turn left at Broughton Street Burwood and proceed to Ian Parade. Turn right at the roundabout at the corner of Dabarita Road, going down to Phillips Street. Prince Edward Park is at the end of this street.

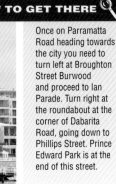

ABOVE: *The water depth off Prince Edward Park is shallow in close and then deepens to about four to five metres.*

LEFT: *Pink nippers make a great bait.*

SNAPSHOT

Platform
GRASSED AREA

Target species
BREAM
DUSKY FLATHEAD
SAND WHITING
LEATHERJACKETS
YELLOWTAIL
SILVER TREVALLY
PAN SIZE SNAPPER
TAILOR
FLOUNDER

Best baits
PRAWNS, PINK NIPPERS, BLOOD WORMS

Best lures
HARDBODIED DEEP DIVERS

Best time
ALL DAY

SEASONS

Bream	**Feb.– May**
Dusky flathead	
Nov.– Apr.	
Sand whiting	**Oct.– Apr.**
Leatherjacket	**Year round**
Yellowtail	**Year round**
Pan sized snapper	
Winter	
Silver trevally	
Mar.– June	
Flounder	**Nov.– Apr.**
Tailor	**Mar– Aug.**

Just around the corner from Cabarita Park is Prince Edward Park which is nestled in the back of Hen and Chicken Bay at Cabarita. This is only a small Sydney park with beautiful views over the bay it is quiet and serene. A walking track links Prince Edward Park to Bayview Park. There is a restaurant situated in the park that you could go for lunch. The restaurant is a newly built federation style building which can cater for weddings and fits in beautifully with the surrounds and has lovely water views over the bay.

TACTICS
To fish here you won't need a rod that is longer than 2.1 metres. Even though this is a very popular fishing spot with the boaties you can still tangle with good-sized bream, whiting and flathead while fishing from shore. When the mullet are freely jumping around in this bay, the bream, flathead and whiting won't be far behind. Early morning surface poppers and walk the dog style lures are great fun. The only problem may be in the landing of the fish as there are a number of hidden snags in the area. I would suggest that you use a beefed up leader of about a metre in length.

BAITS AND LURES
Shallow diving floating lures, lightly weighted soft plastics and 1/8 and 1/4 oz blades will do the trick while fishing here. If you're into bait fishing I would try and fish as light as possible.

BEST TIDE/TIMES
This bay gets very shallow at the bottom of the tide, so I would suggest that you work an hour either side of the top of the tide. This is a good place to come when you are experiencing those Christmas tides as the fish will come in closer to the shore.

AMENITIES
There are picnic shelters, BBQs, children's playground and toilets that also include a disabled toilet. Dogs are allowed on leads. Entry and parking is free but there is a 3 hour parking limit in the car park and all day street parking. There is public transport but the bus does not come directly to the park and there is some walking involved.

KIDS AND FAMILIES
Great place to come for a picnic, even if you are not going to fish.

BAYVIEW PARK

HOW TO GET THERE

Once on Burwood Road at Burwood you will need to travel north along this road for about four kilometres until you reach Bayview Park at the end. There is off street parking here as well as paid parking near the boat ramp.

ABOVE: *Fishing off this wharf is allowed.*

LEFT: *Boat ramps are a great place to fish. Just remember to take your rubbish with you and respect the ramp users.*

SNAPSHOT

Platform
WHARF AND BEACH

Target species
BREAM
DUSKY FLATHEAD
SAND WHITING
LEATHERJACKETS
MULLET
YELLOWTAIL
SILVER TREVALLY
FLOUNDER

Best baits
PILCHARDS, MULLET, BLOOD WORMS, PINK NIPPERS

Best lures
SOFT PLASTICS, BLADES, LIGHTLY WEIGHTED SOFT PLASTICS

Best time
HIGH TIDE

SEASONS

Bream **Feb.– May**
Dusky flathead **Nov.– Apr.**
Sand whiting **Oct.– Apr.**
Leatherjacket **Year round**
Yellowtail **Year round**
Pan sized snapper **Winter**
Silver trevally **Mar.– June**
Flounder **Nov.– Apr.**
Mullet **Year round**

Bayview Park is situated at the end of Burwood Road; this is no ordinary park as it offers far more than merely a playground for children. With spectacular walks overlooking several bays, wharfs and a public boat ramp as well as a BBQ area and picnic tables, this definitely calls for a visit. Bayview Park itself begins with a walk overlooking Exile Bay, which sets the perfect scene for a mosaic sunset if you can arrange to be there just at the right time.

TACTICS

You could try casting a line off the wharf on the run-out tide or you could take a short walk through the park into the back of Hen and Chicken Bay. Here you will come across a small set of mangroves. Try working floating shallow lures over the mangrove roots for bream, flathead and whiting. On the northern side of the park you will find a two laned boat ramp with a pontoon running up the middle. On the left hand side of this ramp there is a small beach, come mud, come rocks area that is worth a cast from the top of the tide and about half way down. You will need to get a decent cast in here to get out past the weed beds.

BAITS AND LURES

Blood worms, pink nippers, peeled prawns, strips of salted slimy mackerel and mullet will do the trick. If you can get hold of some you could also try using chicken and mullet gut soaked in bread crumbs.

BEST TIDE/TIMES

A couple of hours either side of the top of the tide seems to produce more fish, but you should also try near the bottom of the tide. Directing your cast to just over the edge of the weed bed.

AMENITIES

There are barbeques, toilets, a playground, covered picnic tables, plenty of trees to keep the sun off you and a concrete path leading around south-east to Price Edward Park and north-east to Exile Bay. ***NOTE*** – It's illegal to fish on Ferry Wharves during times when the Ferry runs. Check your local wharf for times when fishing is permitted and check if there are any 'No Fishing' signs in the area.

KIDS AND FAMILIES

Plenty for the kids to do if they get sick of fishing they can play in the park, walk along the ferry wharf or just watch the boats come and go at the ramp.

WERRELL RESERVE

HOW TO GET THERE 🔍

Once on Great North Road you will travel along this road for about five kilometres until you come to Werrell Reserve at the end.

ABOVE: *This spot can be fished during the run-in and run-out tides. Fresh bait is a must and don't forget to take those metal lures for the passing schools of tailor.*

LEFT: *Silver trevally frequent this deep water spot.*

SNAPSHOT 🔍

Platform
ROCKS AND BEACH

Target species
BREAM
DUSKY FLATHEAD
SAND WHITING
MULLET
LEATHERJACKETS
YELLOWTAIL
SILVER TREVALLY
PAN SIZE SNAPPER
LUDERICK
FLOUNDER

Best baits
PILCHARDS,
MULLET, BLOOD
WORMS, PINK
NIPPERS

Best lures
SOFT PLASTICS,
BLADES, LIGHTLY
WEIGHTED SOFT
PLASTICS

Best time
HIGH TIDE

SEASONS

Bream	**Feb.– May**
Dusky flathead	
Nov.– Apr.	
Sand whiting	**Oct.– Apr.**
Leatherjacket	**Year round**
Yellowtail	**Year round**
Pan sized snapper	
Winter	
Silver trevally	
Mar.– June	
Flounder	**Nov.– Apr.**
Mullet	**Year round**

Located in Abbotsford at the end of the Great North Road lies Werrell Reserve, home to the 12' Flying Squadron. The Reserve has public toilets, play equipment, tap water and a BBQ for handy amenities for a day in the park. There are a couple of small sandy beaches that you can fish from here.

TACTICS

I would take a couple of rods to fish here. One that would be rigged with a small ball sinker straight down onto the hook and the other outfit would be rigged up to use either a small floating hardbodied lure or a lightly weighted soft plastic.

BAITS AND LURES

Blood worms, pink nippers and the like would get eaten very quickly here by small baitfish. I would tend to use either salted down pilchards, mullet and slimy mackerel strips. You could also try cubing a few pieces of tuna.

BEST TIDE/TIMES

As the water is fairly shallow here I would concentrate my fishing time to about an hour and a half either side of the top of the tide.

AMENITIES

There is running water, toilets, rubbish bins, play equipment, street parking and one barbeque.

KIDS AND FAMILIES

Scenic water views, picnic shelters, BBQ, toilets, play equipment, boat ramp.

CABARITA PARK

HOW TO GET THERE

Once on Majors Bay Road at Concord you will need to turn left at Smythes Street. Proceed along Smythes Street which will change into Cabarita Road. Follow this road down to Cabarita Park. There is plenty of parking here.

SNAPSHOT

Platform
ROCKS AND ROCKWALL

Target species
BREAM
DUSKY FLATHEAD
SAND WHITING
MULLET
LEATHERJACKETS
YELLOWTAIL
SILVER TREVALLY
PAN SIZE SNAPPER
LUDERICK
FLOUNDER
MULLOWAY

Best baits
PILCHARDS, MULLET, BLOOD WORMS AND PINK NIPPERS

Best lures
SOFT PLASTICS, BLADES AND LIGHTLY WEIGHTED SOFT PLASTICS

Best time
MID TO HIGH TIDE

SEASONS

Bream **Feb.– May**
Dusky flathead **Nov.– Apr.**
Sand whiting **Oct.– Apr.**
Leatherjacket **Year round**
Yellowtail **Year round**
Pan sized snapper **Winter**
Silver trevally **Mar.– June**
Flounder **Nov.– Apr.**
Salmon **Mar.– June**
Tailor **Mar. – Aug.**
Mulloway **Oct.– May**
Mullet **Year round**

ABOVE: *On the eastern side of Cabarita Park is another stretch of shoreline that is worth bringing the kids for a fish.*

RIGHT: *Try fishing on either side of the ferry wharf at Cabarita Park from the shore.*

Cabarita Park is a great place to take the family for a picnic, go for a walk, have a fish or just generally chill out and watch the world go by.

TACTICS
When you get here you will find that you will need to put in a decent cast to get out to the more productive water. The depth will vary from 3 to 6 m of water. Many a mulloway have been caught here while fishing the run-out tide. If you are going to chase mulloway here I would suggest that you use a 6 to 10 kg, 3.6 m rod. If you are chasing bream, flathead, whiting and silver trevally here I would use a 4 to 8 kg, 3.6 m rod with a threadline reel that has been spooled with 6 kg line. This would be a good place to have a berley trail going.

BAITS AND LURES
Not a great place to work lures from. I have found it to be mainly a bait fishing area. Try baits, like pink nipper, blood worms, pillie tails and strips of mullet and slimy mackerel. Peeled prawns would also work here, but remember to put a couple of half hitches around the tail of the prawn to stop it flying off when you cast.

BEST TIDE/TIMES
I have found that this spot fish's very well just after there has been a southerly blow and the tide is rising. The bream, flathead and whiting seem to come in closer to feed under the cover of darkness.

You can fish here on a run-out tide, but you will need to cast out further to avoid the snags that are in close to the shore.

AMENITIES
There is plenty of parking here, but there is a fee. At the time of writing it was $12.00 per car. Residents get in free, but it is well worth the cost of the parking fee. There are BBQs, toilets and a play area.

KIDS AND FAMILIES
There is plenty for the kids to do, even if they get sick of fishing.

BREAKFAST POINT

HOW TO GET THERE

Once on Majors Bay Road at Concord head north-west, turn right at Norman Street, right into Richard Street, left into Bradoon Street. Follow this street then turn left into Hilly Street which leads you down to the Putty Ferry and the park at Breakfast Point.

ABOVE: *Limited parking in the street here and the walk through the park and down through the bush can be a bit hard, but this place does produce a few fish at times.*

LEFT: *Don't forget to take a few soft plastics with you when fishing here.*

SNAPSHOT

Platform
SANDSTONE
BREAKWALL

Target species
BREAM
DUSKY FLATHEAD
SAND WHITING
LEATHERJACKETS
YELLOWTAIL
SILVER TREVALLY
PAN SIZE SNAPPER
MULLOWAY
MULLET
TAILOR
FLOUNDER

Best baits
PRAWNS, PINK NIPPERS, BLOOD WORMS

Best lures
HARDBODIED DEEP DIVERS

Best time
ALL DAY, BUT DURING THE HIGHER PARTS OF THE TIDE

Breakfast Point is situated on the downstream side of the ferry in the suburb of Mortlake. It is notable as the former site of the Australian Gas Light Company (AGL) gas works, which is now closed and in the process of redevelopment into the Breakfast Point residential development. There is an elevated walkway on top of a retaining wall that goes around the foreshore in the park. The water depth in close to the wall is fair shallow, but increases to depths that range from 5 to 11 metres.

TACTICS

You could try casting live baits and slabs of mullet, squid and slimy mackerel out towards the moored boats for kingfish, mulloway and flathead. Or you could go to the eastern side of the retaining wall and cast out lightly weighted baits for bream, flathead, whiting, silver trevally and flounder. Leatherjacket can be caught close to the wharfs that are found near the Putty Ferry. Try using a paternoster rig and either small pieces of prawn or squid for bait.

BAITS AND LURES

Blood worms, pink nippers, peeled prawns, strips of salted slimy mackerel and mullet will do the trick. If you can get hold of some you could also try using chicken and mullet gut soaked in bread crumbs.

BEST TIDE/TIMES

A couple of hours either side of the top of the tide seems to produce more fish, but you should also try near the bottom of the tide. Direct your cast to just over the edge of the weed bed.

AMENITIES

There is running water, toilets, rubbish bins, play equipment, street parking and one BBQ. Outlined with trees for shade cover makes it and seclusion makes this a great spot.

KIDS AND FAMILIES

Great place to take the kids and the dogs for a walk, to kick a ball around, ride a bike and of course to go for a fish.

SEASONS

Bream **Feb.– May**
Dusky flathead **Nov.– Apr.**
Sand whiting **Oct.– Apr.**
Leatherjacket, mullet & yellowtail **Year round**
Pan sized snapper **Winter**
Silver trevally **Mar.– June**
Flounder **Nov.– Apr.**
Tailor **Mar. – Aug.**
Mulloway **Oct.– May**

KISSING POINT PARK

HOW TO GET THERE

Travel north across the bridge at Ryde. Once across turn left into Junction Street, then right into Bellmore Street, and right into Morrison Road. This will take you back over Concord Road. Follow this down, turn right into Charles Street and follow it down to the water.

SNAPSHOT

Platform
ESTUARY ROCKS

Target species
BREAM
DUSKY FLATHEAD
SAND WHITING
LEATHERJACKETS
YELLOWTAIL
SILVER TREVALLY
PAN SIZE SNAPPER
TAILOR
FLOUNDER
MULLOWAY

Best baits
PRAWNS, PINK
NIPPERS, BLOOD
WORMS

Best lures
HARD BODIED DEEP
DIVERS

Best time
ALL DAY

SEASONS

Bream **Feb.– May**
Dusky flathead
Nov.– Apr.
Sand whiting **Oct.– Apr.**
Leatherjacket, mullet &
yellowtail **Year round**
Pan sized snapper
Winter
Silver trevally
Mar.– June
Flounder **Nov.– Apr.**
Salmon **Mar.– June**
Tailor **Mar. – Aug.**
Mulloway **Oct.– May**

ABOVE: *Kissing Point Ferry Wharf is worth a shot at night when the ferries are not operating.*

RIGHT: *Try slow rolling those Squidgy soft plastics very slow when targeting mulloway from the shore.*

This park is on the foreshore of the Parramatta River. It is a popular park for events, with River Cat wharf and a boat launching jetty close by. It is part of the Ryde Riverwalk and has a recently upgraded playground and picnic facilities. This area is also part of the Ryde Riverwalk. Care needs to be taken when fishing from the shore here as many a river cat will pass by creating a surge in the water's level. I would suggest that you fish from the ferry wharf, but you could try the floating wharf beside the boat ramp. You will need to remember that the ramp users have the right of way, so you will find yourself winding in a fair bit at times.

TACTICS

Try using a running sinker down onto the swivel with a leader of 1 to 2 m in length. After casting I would suggest that you hold onto the rod as there is a fair amount of current that will run past here at times. If you prefer to cast out your rig and sit it in between the rocks you should try fishing the eastern side of the park on a run-out tide. It does get quite shallow here at low tide.

BAITS AND LURES

Peeled prawns, half pilchards, strips of tuna and salted slimy mackerel. You could also try catching a few poddy mullet in the corner of the bay here and using them for live bait. Soft plastics and blades will work well here and at the top of the tide you could try casting out a few surface lures. You may be surprised at what you get.

BEST TIDE/TIMES

This area can be fished at any part of the tide. You will just need to move around a bit to chase the tide.

AMENITIES

There are picnic areas, BBQs, toilets, sports fields, commuter and recreational cycle path and a walking track/path. The playground features swings, combination equipment, slides and a climbing frame.

KIDS AND FAMILIES

Great place to take the kids for a few hours fishing while at the same time having a picnic. You could also go for a scenic walk.

RYDE RAIL BRIDGE NORTH & SOUTH

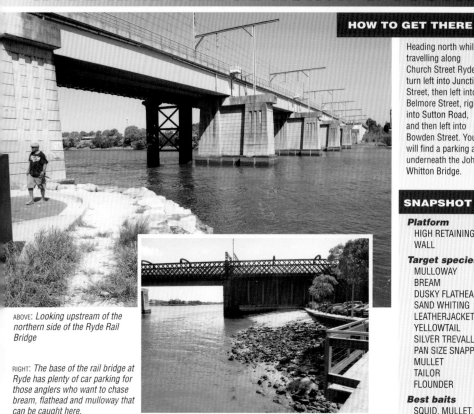

HOW TO GET THERE

Heading north while travelling along Church Street Ryde turn left into Junction Street, then left into Belmore Street, right into Sutton Road, and then left into Bowden Street. You will find a parking area underneath the John Whitton Bridge.

ABOVE: *Looking upstream of the northern side of the Ryde Rail Bridge*

RIGHT: *The base of the rail bridge at Ryde has plenty of car parking for those anglers who want to chase bream, flathead and mulloway that can be caught here.*

There use to be a ramp many years ago beside the rail bridge at Ryde, but it has now been replaced with a sandstone retaining wall and a sandy beach on the downstream side and a sand stone retaining wall on the upstream side. One thing you will need to watch here if fishing off the beach during the lower part of the tide is the swell that is created by the ferries. I have seen many an unsuspecting angler get their feet and gear wet while fishing off this small beach.

TACTICS

Cast soft plastics up current of the bridge base before allowing it to sink to the bottom and then slowly hop it along side of the base. You could also do this with a bait that has a small ball sinker running directly down onto it. When you are using this technique you will need to stay in contact with the line at all times.

BAITS AND LURES

Strips of salted tuna, mullet, slimy mackerel and tuna are the go when it comes to bait. You could also try using those small black crabs that you find under the rocks here. It would be better to use lightly weighted soft plastics or floating diving lures here rather than sinking hardbodied lures and blades.

BEST TIDE/TIMES

Fish on the upstream side on the run-in tide and on the downstream side of the bridge on the run-out tide. Further around into the small bay on the downstream side of the ferry wharf there is an old shed. Try casting from here into the deeper water for bream, flathead, whiting and the odd mulloway.

AMENITIES

There is a small park on the upstream side of the bridge that at the time of writing had a set of toilets in them.

NOTE – It's illegal to fish on Ferry Wharves during times when the Ferry runs. Check your local wharf for times when fishing is permitted and check if there are any 'No Fishing' signs in the area.

KIDS AND FAMILIES

Not a lot to do here for the kids, that is unless they like watching the ferries go up and down the river.

SNAPSHOT

Platform
HIGH RETAINING WALL

Target species
MULLOWAY
BREAM
DUSKY FLATHEAD
SAND WHITING
LEATHERJACKETS
YELLOWTAIL
SILVER TREVALLY
PAN SIZE SNAPPER
MULLET
TAILOR
FLOUNDER

Best baits
SQUID, MULLET, PINK NIPPER, BLOOD WORMS

Best lures
SOFT PLASTICS, BLADES

Best time
TOP OF THE TIDE, EITHER RUN-IN OR RUN-OUT

SEASONS

Bream **Feb.– May**
Dusky flathead & flounder **Nov.– Apr.**
Sand whiting **Oct.– Apr.**
Leatherjacket, mullet & yellowtail **Year round**
Pan sized snapper **Winter**
Silver trevally & salmon **Mar.– June**
Tailor **Mar. – Aug.**
Mulloway **Oct.– May**

SILVERWATER BRIDGE

HOW TO GET THERE

Once on Silverwater Road at Silverwater travel north to turn left at Victoria Road off ramp and then left into Primrose Avenue. At the end of the avenue turn right into John Street. There is parking here and then it is a short walk through Primrose Park. Once you are in the park you will need to walk down stream and under the Silverwater Bridge to the walkway at the water's edge.

SNAPSHOT

Platform
ROCKWALL

Target species
BREAM
DUSKY FLATHEAD
MULLET
SAND WHITING
FLOUNDER

Best baits
SQUID, MULLET, PINK NIPPER, BLOOD WORMS

Best lures
SOFT PLASTICS, BLADES

Best time
TOP OF THE TIDE, EITHER RUN-IN OR RUN-OUT

ABOVE: *It may not look like much, but this is a great place to target bream and flathead.*

LEFT: *A two inch Gulp Shrimp in a Nuclear colour was the undoing of this flathead.*

SEASONS

Bream **Feb.– May**
Dusky flathead **Nov.– Apr.**
Sand whiting **Oct.– Apr.**
Flounder **Nov.– Apr.**
Mullet **Year round**

Silverwater Bridge is one of the major road crossings of the Parramatta River. The bridge carries Silverwater Road traffic over the river to Silverwater in the south to Rydalmere and Ermington in the north. The origin of the suburb's name, and subsequently the bridge's name, is unknown. It may have been a reference to the nearby Parramatta River which could have provided silver reflections of light off the water.

TACTICS

I would suggest you don't bait fish from here, but keep to the lure fishing so that any fish that you do catch from here is released to fight another day. I have caught flathead up to 60 cm here that have not had a tail or pectoral fins. On the other hand the bream that I have caught here have been very silver in colour. Try fishing here for mullet that you are going to use for bait elsewhere.

BAITS AND LURES

Floating shallow lures, surface poppers and walkers are good to use as there are plenty of snags in the water.

BEST TIDE/TIMES

The last hour of the run-in tide and the first hour of the run-out tide.

AMENITIES

None, just a boat ramp and wharf beside it. Watch out at low tide as the ramp and wharf are very slippery.

KIDS AND FAMILIES

Not a lot for the kids to do here.

KING GEORGE PARK – IRON COVE RIVER

HOW TO GET THERE 🔍

Once on City West Link at Lilyfield heading towards the city turn left into Victoria Road, then left into Toelle Street. Once at the end of Toelle turn left into Manning Street.

SNAPSHOT 🔍

Platform
ROCKWALL

Target species
BREAM
DUSKY FLATHEAD
MULLET
SAND WHITING
MULLOWAY
FLOUNDER

Best baits
SQUID, MULLET, PINK NIPPER, BLOOD WORMS

Best lures
SOFT PLASTICS, BLADES

Best time
TOP OF THE TIDE, EITHER RUN-IN OR RUN-OUT

ABOVE: *Great place to fish from a sand stone wall.*

LEFT: *King George Park is a great place to bring the kids for a fish or play on the swing set.*

There is a concrete pathway that winds its way around the shoreline from the bridge and around to Rodd Point. There are a number of restaurants and cafés along the way that you could stop off at for a coffee or an ice-cream. You could easily spend 2 to 3 hours casting out a few lures as you walk around the foreshore.

TACTICS
The stretch of water just out from the park is fairly snaggy, so you will need to get a fair cast in to get over them. Further around the bay, the sea floor changes to deeper water and a good cast will get you out to where a few of the moored boats are. Try using a 1/4 oz blade to get the distance or maybe a soft plastic weighted down with a 1/4 oz jighead. You could always take a short walk to the underside of the bridge and bait fish for bream, flathead, whiting and flounder on the run-out tide. You could try berleying up a few mullet for bait.

BAITS AND LURES
Soft plastics and blades are ideal lures to cast around the area as you can cover plenty of ground.

BEST TIDE/TIMES
High tide would be the best time to work the surface lures and low tide would be a time to try out those heavier weighted soft plastics and blades.

AMENITIES
You will find barbeques, toilets, covered seating, a great playground for the kids, plenty of parking and grassed area for having those family picnics.

KIDS AND FAMILIES
Great place to bring the kids for a walk as there is always something going on.

SEASONS
Bream **Feb.– May**
Dusky flathead **Nov.– Apr.**
Sand whiting **Oct.– Apr.**
Flounder **Nov.– Apr.**
Mulloway **Oct.– May**
Mullet **Year round**

HOW TO GET THERE

Once on Wattle Street at Ashfield continue on into Dobroyd Parade at Dobroyd Point, then turn left into James Street, then turn left into Glover Street. There is a parking area here as well as off street parking.

SNAPSHOT

Platform
ROCK WALL

Target species
BREAM
DUSKY FLATHEAD
MULLET
SAND WHITING
FLOUNDER
MULLOWAY

Best baits
SQUID, MULLET, PINK NIPPER, BLOOD WORMS

Best lures
SOFT PLASTICS, BLADES

Best time
TOP OF THE TIDE, EITHER RUN-IN OR RUN-OUT

There are plenty of spots that you can park your car here and get out and have a cast for bream, flathead, flounder, whiting and the odd tailor.

SEASONS

Bream **Feb.– May**
Dusky flathead **Nov.– Apr.**
Sand whiting **Oct.– Apr.**
Flounder **Nov.– Apr.**
Mulloway **Oct.– May**
Mullet **Year round**

There is a small boat ramp situated just under the bridge at the end of Lilyfield Road. This ramp is not much of a ramp, but at high tide you could try casting an unweighted bait out under the bridge. This is a great place to set a poddy trap on a rising tide.

TACTICS

During the summer months I have been walking along here and noticed plenty of small mullet, garfish and prawns scurrying across the water's surface. It got me to thinking that surface lures and sub-surface lures would work a treat here. You could also try using blades here, but what I would do is change the trebles to singles so that the blade doesn't get caught up as much. Float fishing for garfish and mullet on a rising tide would also be worth a shot, as they come into the shallows with the rising tide.

BAITS AND LURES

Great place to bring someone who wants to learn how to work those surface lures, and surface walkers over weed beds. Try using pink nippers and blood worms for bait. Mullet and chicken gut soaked in tuna oil and covered with bread crumbs will work on the bream and flathead that feed here on a run-out tide.

BEST TIDE/TIMES

High tide would be the best time to work the surface lures and low tide would be a good time to try out those heavier weighted soft plastics and blades.

AMENITIES

Playground, café, bike/skateboard track, toilets, picnic areas, seating, shade.

KIDS AND FAMILIES

A good place to take the kids as there is plenty to do if they get bored with fishing.

HOW TO GET THERE

Once on Wattle Street at Ashfield continue on into Dobroyd Parade at Dobroyd Point. There is a parking area here as well as off street parking.

ABOVE: *Try fishing either side of the Dobroyd Aquatic Club.*

LEFT: *High tide would be the best tide to fish here for bream, flathead, whiting and mullet.*

SNAPSHOT

Platform
ROCKWALL

Target species
BREAM
DUSKY FLATHEAD
MULLET
SAND WHITING
FLOUNDER
MULLOWAY

Best baits
SQUID, MULLET, PINK NIPPER, BLOOD WORMS

Best lures
SOFT PLASTICS, BLADES

Best time
TOP OF THE TIDE, EITHER RUN-IN OR RUN-OUT

Once again there is a concrete walkway that follows the shoreline; making it an easy place to take the kids. You will need to take care as cyclists, joggers and walkers use this area a lot.

TACTICS

Up in the next corner you will come across a bridge. You would think deep water, but not here. It is very shallow at low tide. As you work your way around the bay you will come to a sandstone retaining wall that is about a metre or so above the water. Once again at low tide you will need a decent cast to get over the weed bed. When the tide is high you will be able to work those surface lures and poppers over the weed beds. The bay that is right up in the corner is fairly shallow, but will produce great catches of bream, whiting, mullet and dusky flathead

BAITS AND LURES

Surface lures, poppers and surface walkers worked over the weed beds seems to be the most effective method here.

BEST TIDE/TIMES

High tide would be the best time to work the surface lures and low tide would be a time to try out those heavier weighted soft plastics and blades.

AMENITIES

Playground, café, bike/skateboard track, toilets, picnic areas, seating, shade.

KIDS AND FAMILIES

When the kids lose interest in trying to catch a fish you could always take them over to the park at Rodd Point.

SEASONS

Bream **Feb.– May**
Dusky flathead **Nov.– Apr.**
Sand whiting **Oct.– Apr.**
Flounder **Nov.– Apr.**
Mulloway **Oct.– May**

RODD PARK RODD POINT – IRON COVE RIVER

HOW TO GET THERE

Once on Wattle Street at Ashfield continue on into Dobroyd Parade at Dobroyd Point, then turn left into Timbrell Drive and then continue on into Henley Marine Drive. There is a parking area here as well as off street parking.

SNAPSHOT

Platform
ESTUARY ROCKS AND SAND

Target species
BREAM
FLATHEAD
WHITING
MULLOWAY

Best baits
PINK NIPPERS,
BLOOD WORMS,
MULLET

Best lures
SOFT PLASTICS,
HARDBODIED LURES

Best time
ALL DAY

ABOVE: *Rodd Park at Rodd Point is not the only great land-based spot in this area. Try going for a walk around the foreshore with a spinning outfit and a few lures.*

RIGHT: *Pink soft plastics are a great colour to start with when chasing flathead. But don't forget to have a few extra colours in the bag.*

SEASONS
Bream **Feb.– May**
Dusky flathead **Nov.– Apr.**
Sand whiting **Oct.– Apr.**
Flounder **Nov.– Apr.**
Mulloway **Oct.– May**

Rodd Point has a mixture of rocks and sand, making it a good place to fishing for whiting, bream and flathead. The water is fairly shallow in close, but drops off to about three metres in depth. Anglers will have a fair bit of competition from the yachties who sail from these shores a lot.

TACTICS

This is a place that you take a couple of fold up chairs, the Esky and a couple of rods. The other thing I would take would be a couple of PVC tubes to stick into the sand. The rods would be about 2.1 m in length and both of them would have bait feeder reels mounted on them and spooled with 3 kg braid. Cast out about 20 to 25 m and you will reach water that is about three metres in depth. Sit the rods back into the PVC tubes and sit back and wait for the bait feeder to scream off. If you don't have bait feeder reels you could leave the bail arm open and put a rubber band on the spool to hold the line on. Just make sure that the rubber band is not too tight.

BAITS AND LURES

Blood and tubes worms, pink nippers, salted tuna, mullet and slimy mackerel strips. You could also try using strips of fresh squid. Live poddy mullet will be the undoing of a flathead or two. Blades and soft plastics can be worked out over the edge of the drop-off.

BEST TIDE/TIMES

I would suggest that you fish the area from about three hours either side of the tide if you are fishing with the kids or someone who isn't able to cast a great distance. What you will find here at the bottom half of the tide is that you will have to put in a decent cast to get your lure or bait out past the rocks and snags.

The southern side is better fished when there is a northerly-based wind and vice-versa for the southerly side. This will allow the wind to assist your cast.

AMENITIES

There are BBQs, toilets, covered picnic tables to be found here.

KIDS AND FAMILIES

Good place to bring the kids at high tide as they can also play in the park or on the sandy beach when they get sick of fishing.

SISTERS BAY – IRON COVE RIVER

HOW TO GET THERE

Once on Wattle Street at Ashfield continue on into Dobroyd Parade at Dobroyd Point, then turn left into Timbrell Drive and continue on into Henley Marine Drive until you reach Brett Crescent Park on the left where there is a parking area as well as off street parking.

SNAPSHOT

Platform
ROCKWALL, SANDY BEACHES, MANGROVES.

Target species
BREAM
FLATHEAD
WHITING
MULLET
LEATHERJACKET

Best baits
PINK NIPPERS, MULLET, BLOOD WORMS

Best lures
HARDBODIED LURES, SOFT PLASTICS

Best time
HIGH TIDE

ABOVE: *Just around the corner from Sisters Bay you will find a wharf below the Iron Cove Bridge. Great deep water fishing from here.*

RIGHT: *This fan-tailed leatherjacket took a liking to an ECOGEAR blade.*

One of the most popular harbour side tracks in Sydney, the Iron Cove 'Bay Run' is a social, family-friendly walk in the inner-west. Following the entire natural course of the cove, and never deviating more than 20 m from the water, this flat, well-maintained walk is also bicycle, pram and dog friendly, with lanes for walkers and cyclists clearly marked where possible.

TACTICS

This bay is fairly shallow around the edges, however it does deepen to approximately 3 or 4 m in some places. You could try working around the edges with soft plastics and small floating diving minnows. If you're going to bait fish in close my suggestion is that you use the small ball sinker directly down onto the bait. If you would like to see what you could catch out further you could try using blades up to half an ounce in weight or 4 to 5 inch weighted soft plastics.

BAITS AND LURES

Blades worked with a slow rolling motion. You could also slowly hop them back to the shore. The same techniques would be used with the 4 to 5 inch soft plastics.

BEST TIDE/TIMES

I would class this as mainly a high tide spot as the water does get very shallow in close.

AMENITIES

If you need a cuppa at this point, try the café at Sisters Bay, next to the old Drummoyne swimming pools and the Drummoyne Rowers Club. For toilets you could walk under the bridge and go to Birkenhead Point. This is also a great place to have a feed and look around.

KIDS AND FAMILIES

You could take the kids here as there are a number of things that would keep them interested.

SEASONS

Bream **Feb.– May**
Dusky flathead
Nov.– Apr.
Sand whiting **Oct.– Apr.**
Flounder **Nov.– Apr.**

WOODFORD BAY – LANE COVE RIVER

HOW TO GET THERE

Once on River Road at Riverview you will need to travel to the junction of Longueville Road and Kenneth Street. Turn right here into Kenneth Street then left into Woodford Street. Continue along this street until you come to Kellys Esplanade.

SNAPSHOT

Platform
ROCKWALL.

Target species
BREAM
DUSKY FLATHEAD
MULLET
SAND WHITING
FLOUNDER
MULLOWAY

Best baits
SQUID, MULLET, PINK NIPPER, BLOOD WORMS

Best lures
SOFT PLASTICS, BLADES

Best time
TOP OF THE TIDE, EITHER RUN-IN OR RUN-OUT

SEASONS
Bream **Feb.– May**
Dusky flathead **Nov.– Apr.**
Sand whiting **Oct.– Apr.**
Flounder **Nov.– Apr.**
Mulloway **Oct.– May**

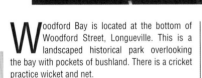

ABOVE: *A dusky flathead just prior to release.*

TOP: *Plenty of room for a number of anglers to fish from this wharf.*

Woodford Bay is located at the bottom of Woodford Street, Longueville. This is a landscaped historical park overlooking the bay with pockets of bushland. There is a cricket practice wicket and net.

TACTICS

The lights at this place will attract squid at night, so don't forget to put in those squid jigs. Try using 2.5 to 3.5 weighted jigs for the best results. The shoreline here fishes well for leatherjacket, whiting, dusky flathead and bream. Work the baits and lures as close as possible to the edge.

BAITS AND LURES

Pilchard, whitebait, frog mouthed pilchards, strips of squid, whole prawns and strips of mullet, tuna and slimy mackerel are worth a shot. Soft plastics can be worked in an umbrella fashion from the shoreline. A cast of about 20 m should do the job.

AMENITIES

Seating is available but there are no toilets. Parking is available for approximately 15 cars. There are some swings for the children. It is a leash free exercise area for dogs.

KIDS AND FAMILIES

Great place for the kids even if they are not into fishing.

TAMBOURINE BAY RESERVE

HOW TO GET THERE

Once on the Pacific Highway you will need to turn left into River Road at Greenwich. Travel for about four kilometres and turn left into Tambourine Road and then travel to the parking at the end of the road.

SNAPSHOT

Platform
ROCKWALL

Target species
BREAM
DUSKY FLATHEAD
MULLET
SAND WHITING
FLOUNDER
MULLOWAY

Best baits
SQUID, MULLET, PINK NIPPER, BLOOD WORMS

Best lures
SOFT PLASTICS, BLADES

Best time
TOP OF THE TIDE, EITHER RUN-IN OR RUN-OUT

This reserve is best fished at high tide, but a long cast will get you out towards the boats that are moored in deeper water.

Tambourine Bay Park is bounded by the southern end of Tambourine Bay Road and Kalloroo Road, Riverview. This is a foreshore park on the edge of Tambourine Bay with a gentle sloping grassed area. It is the start of Tambourine Creek Bushwalks.

TACTICS

You will need to cast a fair distance here in order to avoid the snags that lie at your feet. Tailor and salmon sometimes cruise through here so metal slices and slugs will come in handy when they're around. You could also try working a few soft plastics and blades out wide for flathead, pan sized snapper, silver trevally, bream and the odd mulloway.

BAITS AND LURES

Whole pilchard, garfish, yellowtail, slimy mackerel and mullet would be the best for mulloway and kingfish. Strips of tuna, mullet, slimy mackerel, yellowtail and half pilchards would be the go for the bream, trevally and flathead.

BEST TIDE/TIMES

The time of the tide doesn't really seem to matter here, however, the direction of the wind does. It is not the best place to fish when the wind is coming from the south. The best fishing is during a northerly wind.

AMENITIES

The park has children's play equipment, BBQ facilities and picnic tables and benches. Toilets with disabled access are available. Parking can be found in Tambourine Bay Road and further street parking in Kallaroo Road.

KIDS AND FAMILIES

Not a bad place to bring the family for a few hours of chilling out, while having a BBQ or a picnic.

SEASONS

Bream **Feb.– May**
Dusky flathead **Nov.– Apr.**
Sand whiting **Oct.– Apr.**
Flounder **Nov.– Apr.**
Mulloway **Oct.– May**
Mullet **Year round**

BURNS BAY RESERVE – LANE COVE RIVER

🔍 HOW TO GET THERE

Head north on Burns Bay Road to cross the Fig Tree Bridge. Then travel for about a kilometre to turn right at Penrose Street then veer left into Bridge Street. Turn right into River Road, right into Tambourine Road, then right into Riverview Road. Follow this road until you come to Kooyoung Road. You will find plenty of parking here.

🔍 SNAPSHOT

Platform
GRASSED AREA

Target species
BREAM
DUSKY FLATHEAD
MULLET
SAND WHITING
MULLOWAY
FLOUNDER

Best baits
SQUID, MULLET, PINK NIPPER, BLOOD WORMS

Best lures
SOFT PLASTICS, BLADES

Best time
TOP OF THE TIDE, EITHER RUN-IN OR RUN-OUT

ABOVE: *Great little place to bring the family for a fish.*

RIGHT: *During the cooler months of the year the bream will start to move out of these bays to go to the coast to spawn.*

SEASONS

Bream **Feb.– May**
Dusky flathead **Nov.– Apr.**
Sand whiting **Oct.– Apr.**
Flounder **Nov.– Apr.**
Mulloway **Oct.– May**
Mullet **Year round**

Burns Bay Reserve is a good place to fish when the wind is coming in from the south or east as it is fairly protected here. Care will need to be taken when walking along the rocks and you will need to wear some decent footwear.

TACTICS

A rod between 3 and 3.5 m rated between 4 and 6 kg is ideal when fishing the north-east corner of this point. If you are going to fish on the north-western side I would suggest that you use a paternoster rig. Try berleying with chopped up pilchards. You will need to throw them out about five metres to get over the kelp found here.

BAITS AND LURES

You could try casting a few soft plastics along the beach found here, but don't use them in the enclosed swimming area. Off the rocks you could throw out a few soft plastic jerkbaits on 1/2 oz jigheads or 70 g metal lures. Surface poppers are worth a shot for tailor, salmon and kingfish that patrol along this set of rocks. If you have a southerly wind blowing, try putting a whole pilchard or garfish under a bobby cork for a squid or two.

BEST TIDE/TIMES

Fishing at the top of the tide would be the best time to cast a metal here. If you are bait fishing I would try early in the morning on a falling tide as the sun will be at your back.

AMENITIES

Toilets, children's play equipment and BBQ facilities are available here. A large open grassed area, suitable for playing ball sports, and a tennis practice wall also exist here.

KIDS AND FAMILIES

Great place for the family to come and relax while having a fish or cooking a snag on the BBQ.

CUNNINGHAM REACH PARK

HOW TO GET THERE

Travel south on Centennial Road at Lane Cove and into Burns Bay Road. Proceed past View Street on the left and then watch for the off ramp to the underpass road of the Fig Tree Bridge on the left. It is about 500 m from the Fig Tree Bridge. Drive under the bridge and you will find Cunningham Reach Park on your left.

SNAPSHOT

Platform
GRASSED AREA AND SANDSTONE ROCKS

Target species
BREAM
DUSKY FLATHEAD
MULLET
SAND WHITING
MULLOWAY
FLOUNDER

Best baits
SQUID, MULLET, PINK NIPPERS, BLOOD WORMS

Best lures
SOFT PLASTICS, BLADES

Best time
TOP OF THE TIDE, EITHER RUN-IN OR RUN-OUT

ABOVE: *The shoreline is snaggy in close, but a short cast will get you over them. Flathead, bream and whiting are caught here.*

RIGHT: *It is a personal choice, but I release all my dusky flathead that are over 60cm's. Check out the size of the head. This one measured in at 83cm's.*

This is a small grassed area with sandstone rocks to Lane Cove River, popular with fishermen and picnic parties.

TACTICS

This stretch of shoreline has very deep water close in, so you don't have to cast out far to reach the passing fish. A rod length between 3 and 3.5 m and 4 to 8 kg breaking strain line will do the job of getting a good cast in and lifting the fish out of the water. Spool your reels up with at least six kilogram line. I would use either a paternoster rig or a sinker down onto the swivel with a fluorocarbon leader of 1 to 1.5 m in length.

BAITS AND LURES

Squid, pilchards, prawns, mullet gut, whitebait and frog mouth pilchards would all be well worth the effort. You could also try using blood, tube and beach worms for some of the monster whiting that live here.

BEST TIDE/TIMES

It doesn't seem to matter which part of the tide you fish here. I would concentrate my times to either early mornings or later in the afternoons though.

AMENITIES

There is parking for 15 to 20 cars and is level for wheelchair access. The park has a free gas BBQ and picnic benches and seats. There are no toilets though.

KIDS AND FAMILIES

Great place to take the kids for a few hours as there is plenty for them to do.

SEASONS

Bream	Feb.– May
Dusky flathead	Nov.– Apr.
Sand whiting	Oct.– Apr.
Flounder	Nov.– Apr.
Mulloway	Oct.– May
Mullet	Year round

MOWBRAY PARK – LANE COVE RIVER

🔍 HOW TO GET THERE

Once on Epping Road at Lane Cove North you will need to turn right at Mowbray Road. Then turn left into Avian Crescent.

🔍 SNAPSHOT

Platform
ESTUARY ROCKS

Target species
BREAM
DUSKY FLATHEAD
LUDERICK
MULLET
LEATHERJACKETS
SAND WHITING
MULLOWAY
FLOUNDER

Best baits
SQUID, MULLET, PINK NIPPER, BLOOD WORMS

Best lures
SOFT PLASTICS AND BLADES

Best time
TOP OF THE TIDE, EITHER RUN-IN OR RUN-OUT

ABOVE: *Bream frequent this stretch of the Lane Cove River.*

RIGHT: *Dusky flathead are not frightened to attack a large lure.*

SEASONS

Bream **Feb.– May**
Dusky flathead
Nov.– Apr.
Sand whiting **Oct.– Apr.**
Flounder **Nov.– Apr.**
Mulloway **Oct.– May**
Mullet **Year round**

owbray Park is a beautiful bushland corridor along the Lane Cove River. You can see the mangroves from a boardwalk, and check out sandstone caves. Keep your eye out for animals!

TACTICS

Whole pilchards and garfish rigged on a set of ganged hooks for tailor, salmon, bonito and kingfish that patrol past here. You could also try using half pillies, strips of tuna, bonito and mullet for bream, flathead and pan sized snapper. Don't forget to take a few metal slices and slugs for casting out off the rocks for tailor and salmon. Soft plastics rigged on 1/4 to 3/8 oz jigheads can be worked through the sandy patches found here.

BEST TIDE/TIMES

All of the run-in tide works the best here. This is because you will be able to use the current that

runs past here to take your bait out onto the sandy bottom.

AMENITIES

Toilets, BBQ and parking facilities at the Rotary Memorial Athletic Field.

KIDS AND FAMILIES

Not a bad place to take the family for a few hours to chill out.

CASTLE ROCK RESERVE BEACH

HOW TO GET THERE 🔍

Head north on Spit Road over the Spit Bridge into Manly Road, then right at Sydney Road lights. After about 2 km turn right at the Condamine South Road lights. Turn right into Ernest Street, left at Woodland Street, left into Alder Street, right into Cutler Road, then left into Castle Rock Circuit. Park, and then go down the steps to the beach.

Try fishing in close to the mangroves with lightly weighted baits like peeled prawns, strips of mullet and pillie tails.

SNAPSHOT 🔍

Platform
ESTUARY ROCKS AND BEACH

Target species
BREAM
DUSKY FLATHEAD
LUDERICK, MULLET
LEATHERJACKETS
SAND WHITING
MULLOWAY
FLOUNDER
KINGFISH

Best baits
SQUID, MULLET,
PINK NIPPER,
BLOOD WORMS

Best lures
SOFT PLASTICS,
BLADES

Best time
TOP OF THE TIDE,
EITHER RUN-IN OR
RUN-OUT

E arly European settlement on the peninsula now known as Castlecrag was used by fishermen and boat builders. The suburb now incorporates Australia's most significant and complete urban landscape designs by architect Walter Burley Griffin. Walter named the estate as the prominent rock which reminded him of Castle Rock on which Edinburgh Castle now stands.

TACTICS

This stretch of shoreline has very deep water close in, so you don't have to cast out to far to get to the passing fish. A rod length of somewhere between three to three and a half metres in length and 4 to 8 kg breaking strain will do the job of getting a good cast in and lifting the fish out of the water. Spool your reels up with at least six kilogram line. I would use either the paternoster rig or a sinker down onto the swivel with a fluorocarbon leader of one to one and a half metres in length.

BAITS AND LURES

Squid, pilchards, prawns, mullet gut, whitebait and frog mouth pilchards would be worth a shot. You could also try using blood, tube and beach worms for some of the monster whiting that inhabit the waters here.

BEST TIDE/TIMES

It doesn't seem to matter at which part of the tide that you fish here. I would concentrate my times either during early mornings or later in the afternoon.

AMENITIES

No amenities in the area.

KIDS AND FAMILIES

Great place to go for a picnic, BBQ, swim or a fish with the family.

SEASONS

Bream **Feb.– May**
Dusky flathead &
flounder **Nov.– Apr.**
Sand whiting **Oct.– Apr.**
Leatherjacket, mullet,
squid & yellowtail
Nov.– Apr.
Pan size snapper **Winter**
Silver trevally & salmon
Mar.– June
Tailor **Mar.– Aug.**
Mulloway **Oct.– May**
Kingfish **Nov.– May**

HOW TO GET THERE

Head north along Spit Road and cross the Spit Bridge into Manly Road. Turn left at the light and into Sydney Road, then left into Ethel Street, right into Kanangara Crescent, then left into Peronne Avenue, then right into Sandy Bay Road. There is plenty of parking here.

SNAPSHOT

Platform
BEACH.

Target species
BREAM
DUSKY FLATHEAD
LUDERICK
MULLET
LEATHERJACKETS
SAND WHITING
MULLOWAY
FLOUNDER
SQUID

Best baits
SQUID, MULLET, PINK NIPPER, BLOOD WORMS

Best lures
SOFT PLASTICS, BLADES

Best time
TOP OF THE TIDE, EITHER RUN-IN OR RUN-OUT

SEASONS

Bream **Feb.– May**
Dusky flathead
Nov.– Apr.
Sand whiting **Oct.– Apr.**
Leatherjacket
Year round
Yellowtail **Year round**
Silver trevally
Mar.– June
Flounder **Nov.– Apr.**
Tailor **Mar.– Aug.**
Mulloway **Oct.– May**

Check out the number of moored boats out from Clontarf Beach. Try casting a squid jig out in amongst them.

Clontarf Reserve is one of Sydney's hidden treasures. Located off Sandy Beach Road, Clontarf, the reserve is a must visit for the whole family.

TACTICS

This is a place where you will need to be able to cast out a fair way so that you can get away from the snags at your feet. Tailor and salmon sometimes come in here to chase baitfish too so it pays to have some metal slugs on hand. You could also try working a few soft plastics and blades out wide for flathead, pan sized snapper, silver trevally, bream and the odd mulloway. Try catching a couple of yellowtail or mullet that you can berley up here and use them for live bait for mulloway, flathead and kingfish.

BAITS AND LURES

Whole pilchards, garfish, yellowtail, slimy mackerel and mullet would be the best for mulloway and kingfish. Strips of tuna, mullet, slimy mackerel, yellowtail and half pilchards would be the go for the bream, trevally and flathead.

BEST TIDE/TIMES

The time of the tide doesn't seem to matter here, but the direction of the wind does. Not the best place to fish at when the wind is coming from the south. Better fished during a northerly wind.

AMENITIES

Plenty of amenities available here such as carparks, toilets, BBQs and more.

KIDS AND FAMILIES

Dogs are allowed on a leash in the main area and a short walk down the road is a beach where dogs are allowed without a leash. The park has a kiosk/café which sells great coffee, sandwiches, cakes and some hot food as well as ice-cream and cold drinks. There is also a small restaurant which is available for hire for weddings and functions.

PARRIWI HEAD – MIDDLE HARBOUR

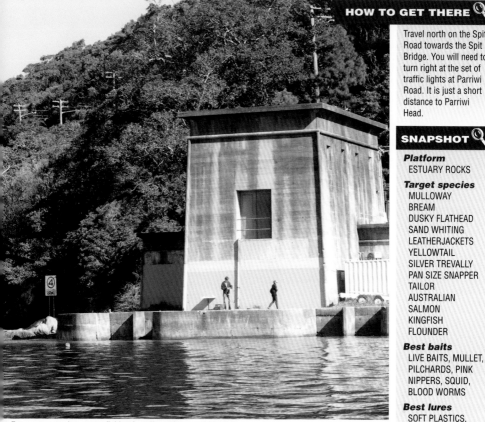

HOW TO GET THERE

Travel north on the Spit Road towards the Spit Bridge. You will need to turn right at the set of traffic lights at Parriwi Road. It is just a short distance to Parriwi Head.

SNAPSHOT

Platform
ESTUARY ROCKS

Target species
MULLOWAY
BREAM
DUSKY FLATHEAD
SAND WHITING
LEATHERJACKETS
YELLOWTAIL
SILVER TREVALLY
PAN SIZE SNAPPER
TAILOR
AUSTRALIAN SALMON
KINGFISH
FLOUNDER

Best baits
LIVE BAITS, MULLET, PILCHARDS, PINK NIPPERS, SQUID, BLOOD WORMS

Best lures
SOFT PLASTICS, BLADES, SURFACE POPPERS, METAL SLICES

Best time
EARLY MORNING & LATE AFTERNOON AT THE TOP OF THE TIDE

Easy access to deep water fishing for tailor, salmon and kingfish.

Parriwi Head Light, also known as Rosherville Light and Port Jackson Entrance Range Rear Light, is an active lighthouse located just off Parriwi Road, near Rosherville Reserve on the south side of Middle Harbour in Mosman. It serves as the rear range light with Grotto Point Light serving as the front light into Port Jackson. Grotto Point Light is located almost exactly 1.6 km in front of Parriwi Head Light.

TACTICS

This stretch of shoreline has very deep water close in, so you don't have to cast out to far to get to the passing fish. A rod in the 3 to 3.5 m range and 4 to 8 kg breaking strain will do the job of getting a good cast in and lifting the fish out of the water. Spool your reels up with at least six kilogram line. I would use either the paternoster rig or a sinker down onto the swivel with a fluorocarbon leader of 1 to 1.5 m in length.

BAITS AND LURES

Squid, pilchards, prawns, mullet gut, whitebait and frog mouth pilchards would be worth a shot. You could also try using blood, tube and beach worms for some of the monster whiting that live here.

BEST TIDE/TIMES

It doesn't seem to matter at which part of the tide that you fish here. I would concentrate my times on either early mornings or later in the afternoon.

AMENITIES

You will need to go to the local shopping centre.

KIDS AND FAMILIES

There is a lot of history at this place, so it would be a good place to take the kids to find out about local knowledge of the place. While there I would have a good look around at the number of great fishing spots that are here. The next time you come back you will have a rod in your hand.

SEASONS

Bream **Feb.– May**
Dusky flathead & flounder **Nov.– Apr.**
Sand whiting **Oct.– Apr.**
Leatherjacket & yellowtail **Year round**
Silver trevally & salmon **Mar.– June**
Flounder **Nov.– Apr.**
Tailor **Mar.– Aug.**
Mulloway **Oct.– May**
Luderick **Mar.– Sep.**
Kingfish **Nov.– May**

SPIT BRIDGE – MIDDLE HARBOUR

HOW TO GET THERE

Go south along the Burnt Bridge Creek Deviation into Manly Road at Balgowlah towards the Spit Bridge. Cross the lights at Sydney Road and under a road bridge. Going down the hill you turn off to the left into Avona Crescent.

SNAPSHOT

Platform
ROCKWALL

Target species
MULLOWAY, BREAM
DUSKY FLATHEAD
SAND WHITING
LEATHERJACKETS
YELLOWTAIL
SILVER TREVALLY
PAN SIZE SNAPPER
SQUID, TAILOR
AUSTRALIAN SALMON
KINGFISH, FLOUNDER

Best baits
LIVE BAITS,
YELLOWTAIL, SLIMY
MACKEREL, PRAWNS,
PINK NIPPERS,
MULLET

Best lures
SURFACE POPPERS,
BLADES, SOFT
PLASTICS

Best time
A COUPLE HOURS
EITHER SIDE OF TOP &
BOTTOM OF THE TIDE

SEASONS

Bream **Feb.– May**
Dusky flathead &
flounder **Nov.– Apr.**
Sand whiting **Oct.– Apr.**
Leatherjacket, mullet,
squid & yellowtail
Year round
Pan sized snapper &
John Dory **Winter**
Silver trevally & salmon
Mar.– June
Flounder **Nov.– Apr.**
Tailor **Mar.– Aug.**
Mulloway **Oct.– May**
Luderick **Mar.– Sep.**
Kingfish **Nov.– May**

Plenty of land-based possies here.

The Spit Bridge is a bascule bridge that carries Spit Road over Middle Harbour in Sydney, New South Wales, Australia, at a point called 'The Spit', 10 km north-east of the CBD. It connects the suburbs of Mosman on the south bank and Seaforth on the north bank.

TACTICS

Not a bad place to fish when the wind is coming in from the south or east as it is fairly protected here. Care will need to be taken when walking along the rocks and you will need to wear some decent footwear. Try berleying with chopped up pilchards. You will need to throw them out about five metres to get over the kelp found here.

BAITS AND LURES

You could try casting a few soft plastics along the beach found here, but don't use them in the enclosed swimming area. Off the rocks you could throw out a few Gulp! Jerkbaits on 1/2 oz jigheads or 70 G metal lures. Surface poppers are worth a shot for tailor, salmon and kingfish that patrol along this set of rocks. If you have a southerly wind blowing, try putting a whole pilchard or garfish under a bobby cork for a squid or two.

BEST TIDE/TIMES

Fishing at the top of the tide would be the best time to cast a metal or slug type lure or two here. If you are bait fishing I would try early in the morning on a falling tide as the sun will be at your back.

AMENITIES

No amenities in the immediate area.

KIDS AND FAMILIES

The water here is very deep and does run very fast at times. There are plenty of snags in close, so anyone fishing here will need to be able to cast out a fair bit to get away from the snags.

THE SPIT RESERVE – MIDDLE HARBOUR

HOW TO GET THERE

Travel north on the Spit Road at the Spit Junction towards the Spit Bridge. Turn left into the paid car park that is situated just after the set of traffic lights at the bottom of the hill.

ABOVE: *Plenty of space to walk along and cast a lure or two.*

RIGHT: *At low tide you can walk along the narrow beach and cast out lightly weighted bait for bream and flathead.*

Evidence of Aboriginal activity has been found on the foreshore and ridge sites of Middle Harbour, especially from Pearl Bay to Quakers Hat Park. Since the first land grant over The Spit Reserves in 1811, land comprising The Spit Reserves has been used for farming, a pleasure garden, the base for a punt service across Middle Harbour, a sandstone quarry, swimming baths, and a sewerage syphon. There is a sandy beach plus grassed area on which commercial boating and food and beverage developments are located at intervals.

TACTICS

This stretch of shoreline has very deep water close in, so you don't have to cast out too far to get to the passing fish. A rod length of somewhere between 3 and 3.5 m in length and four to eight kilo breaking strain will do the job of getting a good cast in and lifting the fish out of the water. Spool your reels up with at least six kilogram line. I would use either the paternoster rig or a sinker down onto the swivel with a fluorocarbon leader of 1 to 1.5 m in length.

BAITS AND LURES

Whole pilchards and garfish rigged on a set of ganged hooks for tailor, salmon, bonito and kingfish that patrol past here. You could also try using half pillies, strips of tuna, bonito and mullet for bream, flathead and pan sized snapper. Don't forget to take a few metal slices and slugs for casting out off the rocks for tailor and salmon.

BEST TIDE/TIMES

All of the run-in tide works the best here. This is because you will be able to use the current that runs past here to take your bait out onto the sandy bottom.

AMENITIES

Picnic, BBQ facilities, amenities building, car park (parking fee required), Mosman Rowing Club, dinghy storage racks, pathways, pontoon and a sea wall.

KIDS AND FAMILIES

Great place to bring the kids. It is not all about the fishing as there is plenty for them to see and do here.

SNAPSHOT

Platform
RETAINING WALL

Target species
MULLOWAY, BREAM
DUSKY FLATHEAD
SAND WHITING
LEATHERJACKETS
YELLOWTAIL
SILVER TREVALLY
PAN SIZE SNAPPER
SQUID, TAILOR
AUSTRALIAN SALMON
KINGFISH, FLOUNDER

Best baits
LIVE BAITS,
YELLOWTAIL, SLIMY
MACKEREL, PRAWNS,
PINK NIPPERS,
MULLET

Best lures
SURFACE POPPERS,
BLADES, SOFT
PLASTICS

Best time
A COUPLE HOURS
EITHER SIDE OF TOP &
BOTTOM OF THE TIDE

SEASONS

Bream **Feb.– May**
Dusky flathead &
flounder **Nov.– Apr.**
Sand whiting **Oct.– Apr.**
Leatherjacket, mullet,
squid & yellowtail
Year round
Pan sized snapper
Winter
Silver trevally & salmon
Mar.– June
Tailor **Mar.– Aug.**
Mulloway **Oct.– May**
Luderick **Mar.– Sep.**
Kingfish **Nov.– May**

BEAUTY POINT PARK – MIDDLE HARBOUR

HOW TO GET THERE

From the Spit Junction travel north on Spit Road towards the Spit Bridge and turn left at the lights into Pearl Bay Avenue. Travel along this road and into Beauty Point Street. Find a parking spot and proceed to the walking track at the water's edge.

SNAPSHOT

Platform
ROCKS

Target species
BREAM
DUSKY FLATHEAD
LUDERICK
MULLET
LEATHERJACKETS
SAND WHITING
MULLOWAY
FLOUNDER

Best baits
LIVE BAITS,
YELLOWTAIL,
SLIMY MACKEREL,
PRAWNS, PINK
NIPPERS, MULLET

Best lures
SURFACE POPPERS,
BLADES AND SOFT
PLASTICS

Best time
A COUPLE HOURS
EITHER SIDE OF TOP
& BOTTOM OF TIDE

SEASONS
Bream **Feb.– May**
Dusky flathead &
flounder **Nov.– Apr.**
Sand whiting **Oct.– Apr.**
Leatherjacket, mullet,
squid & yellowtail
Year round
Pan sized snapper
Winter
Silver trevally & salmon
Mar.– June
Tailor **Mar.– Aug.**
Mulloway **Oct.– May**
Luderick **Mar.– Sep.**
Kingfish **Nov.– May**

ABOVE: *Try working the shoreline from here and up stream. Lightly weighted pillie tails or peeled prawns are the go.*

LEFT: *Remember to berley when fishing from here for the best results.*

This is just one section of a beautiful walk around Sydney Harbour. You have to use some surface roads in parts but mostly it's along a well-maintained track by the water's edge. Spectacular views. An early morning walk is fresh and peaceful and you can finish up at Chowder Bay or up top at Middle Head for breakfast.

TACTICS

During the summer months many a mulloway, snapper and big dusky flathead have been caught here. You will need to get a decent cast in here to get your rig out past the kelp and snags. Try using a number 5 to 6 ball sinker that slides down onto the bait or the paternoster rig. During the autumn to winter months you will be in with a good chance of catching luderick on cabbage or weed. I would suggest that you use a mixture of bread, sand and chopped up weed and cabbage for berley for the luderick. One of those stemmed floats will do the trick, no need to use a bobby cork here. It is also worth having a few squid jigs and metal lures in the bag during the cooler months of the year.

BAITS AND LURES

Squid, pilchards, prawns, mullet gut and strips, whitebait and frog mouth pilchards would be worth a shot. You could also try using blood, tube and beach worms for some of the monster whiting that live here.

BEST TIDE/TIMES

It doesn't seem to matter which part of the day that you fish here. I would concentrate my times around early mornings or later in the afternoon.

AMENITIES

The closest amenities would be in the nearby shopping centre.

KIDS AND FAMILIES

Not a lot to do here that is unless your kids are into exploring around the rocks and fishing.

PRIMROSE PARK – MIDDLE HARBOUR

HOW TO GET THERE

Primrose Park, Grafton Street (off Young Street), Cremorne, has a designated car park in the park, and limited on-street parking. It is a 10 minute walk to Military Road and numerous bus stops.

SNAPSHOT

Platform
GRASSED AREA & ROCKS

Target species
MULLOWAY, BREAM
DUSKY FLATHEAD
SAND WHITING
LEATHERJACKETS
YELLOWTAIL
SILVER TREVALLY
PAN SIZE SNAPPER
TAILOR, SQUID
MULLET
AUSTRALIAN SALMON
KINGFISH, FLOUNDER

Best baits
LIVE BAITS, MULLET,
PILCHARDS, PINK
NIPPERS, SQUID,
BLOOD WORMS

Best lures
SOFT PLASTICS,
BLADES, SURFACE
POPPERS, METAL
SLICES

Best time
EARLY MORNING AND
LATE AFTERNOON AT
THE TOP OF THE TIDE

ABOVE: *As you will see it is very snaggy here at low tide. Try working small surface lures here in the summer months at the top of the tide.*

LEFT: *Work those soft plastics during the top of the tide for flathead and bream from here.*

BAITS AND LURES

Try using baits like pink nippers, beach and blood worms, whole and peeled prawns, and strips of mullet, mullet and chicken gut and don't forget to try whitebait.

BEST TIDE/TIMES

As the water is not as deep as many other shore-based spots in Middle Harbour I would suggest that you fish the top half of the tide. The weekends can get extremely busy here so I would try and concentrate on early mornings and late afternoons on the weekend and during the whole day throughout the week.

AMENITIES

The sports fields cater for football, hockey and cricket, as well as for training, school sport and carnivals. There are tennis courts, cricket nets, flood lights, change rooms, toilets and hockey and tennis club houses.

KIDS AND FAMILIES

A bush walking track connects to Folly Point, and a circuit walk from Willoughby Falls up to Grafton Street returns via the zig-zag track. Across the road, Brightmore Reserve has a tricycle track and is a great picnic spot. Dogs are welcome in Primrose Park; however, they are not permitted on the sports fields when organised sport is being played and they must be kept on a leash in bushland areas.

Historical items and sites including Aboriginal rock art indicate that Primrose Park was frequented by the Cammeraygal people. Originally an estuarine bay, in 1899 the land on which the sports fields now stand became the site of North Sydney's first sewage treatment works. The sewage works closed in the late 1920s and the area was dedicated as parkland in 1930. The Park was named after HL Primrose, Mayor of North Sydney from 1926 to 1932, and later NSW Minister for Health. One of North Sydney's premier sportsgrounds and a significant area of urban bushland. Located on the foreshores of Willoughby Bay, the Park is popular with both local residents and visitors due to its mix of sporting and other recreational facilities.

TACTICS

The outfit should be either a 1 to 3 or 2 to 4 kg outfit, that the reel has been spooled with 3 kg braid. These outfits could be used for both bait and lure fishing. You will need to decide which one you would prefer to fish with. If you are bait fishing I would suggest you fish as light as the conditions will allow.

SEASONS

Bream **Feb.– May**
Dusky flathead &
flounder **Nov.– Apr.**
Sand whiting **Oct.– Apr.**
Leatherjacket, mullet,
squid & yellowtail
Year round
Pan sized snapper
Winter
Silver trevally & salmon
Mar.– June
Tailor **Mar.– Aug.**
Mulloway **Oct.– May**
Luderick **Mar.– Sep.**
Kingfish **Nov.– May**

TUNKS PARK – MIDDLE HARBOUR

HOW TO GET THERE

Once on Millers Street North Sydney proceed along the street until it turns into Strathallen Avenue. Then turn right at Marana Road then travel down and into Lower Cliff Avenue. You will come to a large parking area at the base of the hill which is Tunks Park

ABOVE: *This is definitely a high tide spot. Fish with lightly weighted baits.*

LEFT: *Try working hard bodied lures around the shoreline here, especially near the cleaning table.*

SNAPSHOT

Platform
RETAINING WALL AND RAMP

Target species
BREAM
FLATHEAD
WHITING
MULLET
GARFISH
SILVER TREVALLY
LEATHERJACKETS
MULLOWAY
KINGFISH

Best baits
LIVE BAITS, MULLET, PILCHARDS, PINK NIPPERS, SQUID, BLOOD WORMS

Best lures
SOFT PLASTICS, BLADES, SURFACE POPPERS, METAL SLICES

Best time
EARLY MORNING AND LATE AFTERNOON AT THE TOP OF THE TIDE

SEASONS

Bream **Feb.– May**
Dusky flathead & flounder **Nov.– Apr.**
Sand whiting **Oct.– Apr.**
Leatherjacket & yellowtail **Year round**
Pan sized snapper **Winter**
Silver trevally & slimy mackerel **Mar.– June**
Mulloway **Oct.– May**
Kingfish **Nov.– May**

The most compelling aspect of Tunks Park lies hundreds of metres above: the famous stone Suspension Bridge at Northbridge. From the North Sydney CBD, it is possible to drive along Miller Street towards Northbridge. In order to access Tunks Park, it is necessary to drive across the beautiful old bridge, whose road is Strathallen Avenue. Once across the bridge, turn right onto Cliff Avenue, then drive down to Tunks Park along Lower Cliff Avenue.

TACTICS
The lights at this place will attract squid at night, so don't forget to pack those squid jigs. Try using 2.5 to 3.5 weighted jigs for the best results. The shoreline here fishes well for leatherjacket, whiting, dusky flathead and bream. Work the baits and lures as close as possible to the edge.

BAITS AND LURES
Pilchard, whitebait, frog mouthed pilchards, strips of squid, whole prawns and strips of mullet, tuna and slimy mackerel are worth a shot. Soft plastics can be worked in an umbrella fashion from the shoreline. A cast of about 20 m would do the job.

BEST TIDE/TIMES
The weekends get extremely busy here, as you can have sporting events, walkers, shorebased anglers and boaties. Try coming here during the week, or on very overcast days during winter when many people are by the fire.

AMENITIES
There are other man-made features of the park that may be of interest to prospective visitors, including a sports field, boat ramp, BBQs and exercise equipment. There is also a playground that is designed to blend in with the natural environment – complete with a tree house, seesaw, spring-mounted deck and a large gravel pit. There is even provision made for wheelchair users, with a large curved access ramp that was added to the park in 1996.

KIDS AND FAMILIES
Tunks Park is a recreation area, popular among joggers and those wishing to walk their dogs. It also supports three sporting fields, notable cricket pitches during the summer, soccer, rugby league and union fields during the winter.

CLIVE PARK – MIDDLE HARBOUR

HOW TO GET THERE

Once on the Pacific Highway at Artarmon turn right at Mowbray road and travel about three kilometres then turn right into Alpha Road. Proceed to Sailors Bay Road at Northbridge where you turn left. Travel about two kilometres until you reach Clive Park.

ABOVE: *There are a number of spots you can fish from the point to the sailing shed for bream, whiting, flathead and trevally.*

RIGHT: *There is a small picnic area half way down to the shore.*

SNAPSHOT

Platform
GRASSED AREA AND BEACH

Target species
MULLOWAY
BREAM
DUSKY FLATHEAD
SAND WHITING
LEATHERJACKETS
YELLOWTAIL
SILVER TREVALLY
PAN SIZE SNAPPER
SQUID
TAILOR
FLOUNDER

Best baits
SQUID, MULLET, PINK NIPPER, BLOOD WORMS

Best lures
SOFT PLASTICS, BLADES

Best time
TOP OF THE TIDE, EITHER RUN-IN OR RUN-OUT

Sydney's harbour coastline is rich with foreshore parks and beaches and each of them serves as a relaxing picnic spot. Northbridge is a suburb in the north shore that is essentially a residential area featuring unique waterfronts. A popular park here is Clive park, located at the corner of Sailors Bay and Coolawin Roads sweeping down to the foreshore of Middle Harbour.

TACTICS

This stretch of shoreline has very deep water close in, so you don't have to cast out too far to get to the passing fish. A rod length of somewhere between 3 and 3.5 m in length and four to eight kilo breaking strain will do the job of getting a good cast in and lifting the fish out of the water. Spool your reels up with at least six kg line. I would use either the paternoster rig or a sinker down onto the swivel with a fluorocarbon leader of 1 to 1.5 m in length.

BAITS AND LURES

Squid, pilchards, prawns, mullet gut and strips, whitebait and frog mouth pilchards would be worth a shot. You could also try using blood, tube and beach worms for some of the monster whiting that live here.

BEST TIDE/TIMES

It doesn't seem to matter which part of the tide that you fish here. I would concentrate my times to either early mornings or later in the afternoon.

AMENITIES

While you are fishing your family and friends can enjoy their time at the park which offers other facilities like a small sheltered beach suitable for children, swings and playgrounds (set in the park bushland), picnic areas and wonderful harbour views to supplement it all.

KIDS AND FAMILIES

There is plenty here for the family and the kids to do besides fishing.

SEASONS

Bream **Feb.– May**
Dusky flathead &
flounder **Nov.– Apr.**
Sand whiting **Oct.– Apr.**
Leatherjacket, yellowtail, mullet, garfish & squid
Year round
Pan sized snapper
Winter
Silver trevally
Mar.– June
Mulloway **Oct.– May**
Tailor **Mar.– Aug**

SAILORS BAY PARK – MIDDLE HARBOUR

HOW TO GET THERE

From the Pacific Highway at Artarmon turn right at Mowbray road and travel about three kilometres to turn left into Alpha Road, then right into Edinburgh Road. Proceed until you come to Sortie Port and turn right. Turn left into The Bastion, left again into The Scarp, then right into Rockley Street.

SNAPSHOT

Platform
ROCKS

Target species
FLATHEAD
BREAM
WHITING
MULLET
MULLOWAY
SILVER TREVALLY
TAILOR
AUSTRALIAN SALMON
KINGFISH
PAN SIZED SNAPPER

Best baits
SQUID, MULLET, PINK NIPPER, BLOOD WORMS

Best lures
SOFT PLASTICS, BLADES

Best time
TOP OF THE TIDE, EITHER RUN-IN OR RUN-OUT

SEASONS

Bream **Feb.– May**
Dusky flathead & flounder **Nov.– Apr.**
Sand whiting **Oct.– Apr.**
Leatherjacket, yellowtail, mullet, & squid
Year round
Pan sized snapper
Winter
Silver trevally & salmon
Mar.– June
Mulloway **Oct.– May**
Tailor **Mar.– Aug**
Kingfish **Nov.– May**

ABOVE: *The view from across Sailors Bay to the sailing club at Clive Park.*

LEFT: *Work the shoreline here with either fresh bait or lures.*

This 1.5 km return walk leads to Sailors Bay. As you traverse along Sailors Bay Creek you will enter a majestic Coachwood Forest. The track reveals a hidden waterfall and beautiful sandstone rock formations. A circuit walk can be achieved by walking up the 'coachwood steps' to Casement Reserve and then returning along the Redoubt and The Rampart. The Griffin Federation Track links back to The Outpost. The grade of this track leading down to the water is medium with steep sandstone steps.

TACTICS

During the summer months many a mulloway, snapper and big dusky flathead have been caught here. You will need to get a decent cast in here to get your rig out pass the kelp and snags. Try using a number 5 or 6 ball sinker that slides down onto the bait or the paternoster rig. During the autumn to winter months you will be in with a good chance of catching luderick on cabbage or weed. I would suggest that you use a mixture of bread, sand and chopped up weed and cabbage for berley for the luderick. One of those stemmed floats will do the trick, no need to use a bobby cork here. It is also worth having a few squid jigs and metal lures in the bag during the cooler months of the year.

BAITS AND LURES

You can catch your own live yellowtail and squid here, but you will need to work hard at it. Whole dead fish like yellowtail, slimy mackerel, mullet and garfish will also attract a mulloway or two while fishing here. Strips of squid, tuna, mullet and bonito are a great bait for trevally, bream and flathead that can be caught here on the rising tide.

BEST TIDE/TIMES

I have found that this spot fish's very well just after there has been a southerly blow and the tide is rising. The bream, flathead and whiting seem to come in closer to feed under the cover of darkness. You can fish here on a run-out tide, but you will need to cast out further to avoid the snags that are in close to the shore.

AMENITIES

There are plenty of toilets on the reserve and BBQs.

KIDS AND FAMILIES

The reserve is a popular Sunday picnic destination as it has BBQs and other facilities. It also has one of the more extensive grassy slopes on Sydney Harbour and is popular for fishing or just to lie down and watch the boats and yachts as they go by.

HOW TO GET THERE

Once on Eastern Valley Way at Willoughby you will need to turn right into Cawarrah Road, then right into Rembrandt Drive. About 500 m along this drive you will need to turn off to your right into a loop road that goes through Harold Reid Reserve.

SNAPSHOT

Platform
ROCK WALLS, ESTUARY ROCKS AND SANDY BEACHES

Target species
MULLOWAY
BREAM
DUSKY FLATHEAD
SAND WHITING
LEATHERJACKETS
YELLOWTAIL
SILVER TREVALLY
PAN SIZE SNAPPER
TAILOR
FLOUNDER

Best baits
SQUID, MULLET, PINK NIPPER, BLOOD WORMS

Best lures
SOFT PLASTICS, BLADES

Best time
TOP OF THE TIDE, EITHER RUN-IN OR RUN-OUT

SEASONS
Bream **Feb.– May**
Dusky flathead & flounder **Nov.– Apr.**
Sand whiting **Oct.– Apr.**
Leatherjacket & yellowtail **Year round**
Pan sized snapper **Winter**
Silver trevally **Mar.– June**
Tailor **Mar.– Aug**
Mulloway **Oct.– May**

Hard spot to get to, but well worth it in the end.

This 36.9 ha reserve comprises the eastern end of the Middle Cove peninsula. Comprising one of the North Shore's finest areas of natural bushland, the land known as Sugarloaf Reserve was transferred from the Cumberland Country Council to Willoughby Council in 1960. It was renamed Harold Reid Reserve in honour of the long-standing Willoughby town clerk Harold James Reid and it was officially opened on 8 May 1965.

TACTICS
Fish in close with a stemmed float for luderick. You need to berley to keep them around your float. You will need to find either green weed or cabbage elsewhere and bring it in with you as there is very little on the rocks. Also, due to the fact that the wall is a fair bit off the water you will need to bring a long handled landing net with you. Once you have caught a fish you can keep them fresh by putting them into a bucket or hang a keeper net over the side of the wall. Just keep an eye out for rats that will take a liking to your fish.

BAITS AND LURES
Surface poppers and large soft plastics can be worked here either early in the morning or just before the sun sets. When there has been a lot of fresh water from a flood you could try using floating deep divers for a mulloway or two. Half and one ounce blades can be hopped over the bottom here, but you will need to judge it right when you make the last lift as you can easily get snagged up close into the rocks.

BEST TIDE/TIMES
You will find that the eastern side of this point is fished the most. Therefore the run-out tide would be the best time to fish from here as your baits and rigs will stay away from the snags that are in close. During the cooler months of the year the luderick will school up here and quite often it can be shoulder-to-shoulder fishing when they're on the chew.

AMENITIES
Picnic facilities, including gas BBQs, and toilets are available in the car parking area.

KIDS AND FAMILIES
There is a fair walk to get to this spot, but most kids will make it.

GARIGAL NP – MIDDLE HARBOUR

HOW TO GET THERE

Once on the Wakehurst Parkway you will need to turn left into Warringah Road. Travel along this road for about five kilometres until you turn off to the left to the Healey toll booth. Drive to the car park at the end and remember to pay your parking fee.

ABOVE: *Great place to bring the kids.*

SNAPSHOT

Platform
ROCK WALLS, ESTUARY ROCKS AND SANDY BEACHES

Target species
MULLOWAY
BREAM
DUSKY FLATHEAD
SAND WHITING
LEATHERJACKETS
YELLOWTAIL
SILVER TREVALLY
PAN SIZE SNAPPER
TAILOR
FLOUNDER

Best baits
SQUID, MULLET, PINK NIPPER AND BLOOD WORMS

Best lures
SOFT PLASTICS AND BLADES

Best time
TOP OF THE TIDE, EITHER RUN-IN OR RUN-OUT

SEASONS
Bream **Feb.– May**
Dusky flathead **Nov.– Apr.**
Sand whiting **Oct.– Apr.**
Leatherjacket, mullet, garfish & yellowtail **Year round**
Silver trevally **Mar.– June**
Flounder **Nov.– April**
Mulloway **Oct.– May**

LEFT: *Work the deep water found off here with blades. The only problem you may come across is those blade eating rocks.*

Garigal National Park is a national park in NSW, 20 km north of central Sydney. The park is somewhat disjointed but covers the following areas: Bantry Bay between the suburbs of Killarney Heights and Forestville to the West and Wakehurst Parkway (and Manly Dam Reserve) to the east. Along Middle Harbour and Middle Harbour Creek between (to the west) the suburbs of Killarney Heights, Forestville, French's Forest, Davidson, Belrose and (to the east) the suburbs of East Lindfield, East Killara, St Ives, as far North as Mona Vale Road (where it abuts Ku-ring-gai Chase National Park). To the South of Mona Vale Road the Park runs as far east as the suburb of Elanora and Narrabeen Lagoon.

TACTICS

During the summer months many a mulloway, snapper and big dusky flathead have been caught here. You will need to get a decent cast in here to get your rig out pass the kelp and snags. Try using a number 5 to 6 ball sinker that slides down onto the bait or the paternoster rig. During the autumn to winter months you will be in with a good chance of catching luderick on cabbage or weed. I would suggest that you use a mixture of bread, sand and chopped up weed and cabbage for berley for the luderick. One of those stemmed floats will do the trick, no need to use a bobby cork here. It is also worth having a few squid jigs and metal lures in the bag during the cooler months of the year.

BAITS AND LURES

Live baits like blood worms, pink nippers, poddy mullet, garfish and yellowtail would have to be the prime baits for when fishing from the shoreline. Just up the road at Drummoyne Bait and Tackle you can get a few of these live baits.

BEST TIDE/TIMES

As this is a fairly shallow bay the best time to fish from the shore here would be during the run-up tide. You could also fish the first hour of the run-out tide. The wind can swirl around in this bay a fair bit, so I would check out the strength of the wind before coming here to fish. A light breeze would be the best.

AMENITIES

There are plenty of toilets and BBQs in the reserve.

KIDS AND FAMILIES

The reserve is a popular Sunday picnic destination as it has BBQ and other facilities. It also has one of the more extensive grassy slopes on Sydney Harbour and is popular for fishing or just to lie down and watch the boats and yachts as they go by.

KILLARNEY POINT – MIDDLE HARBOUR

HOW TO GET THERE

Go north on Warringah Road and turn right onto Melwood Avenue to Downpatrick Road on the right. Turn left into Killarney Drive. Drive to the end of this road and find a parking spot near here. Walk to the end of the road to find the Flat Rock Walking track. It is about a 30 minute walk to the shore.

ABOVE: *Even though you have to pay to park here there is plenty on offer for the land-based angler.*

RIGHT: *Bream and flathead can be caught from beside the boat ramp here. Just remember to respect the boat owners.*

SNAPSHOT

Platform
ROCK WALLS, ESTUARY ROCKS AND SANDY BEACHES

Target species
MULLOWAY, BREAM DUSKY FLATHEAD SAND WHITING LEATHERJACKETS YELLOWTAIL, SQUID SILVER TREVALLY PAN SIZE SNAPPER TAILOR, FLOUNDER

Best baits
SQUID, MULLET, PINK NIPPER, BLOOD WORMS

Best lures
SOFT PLASTICS, BLADES

Best time:
TOP OF THE TIDE, EITHER RUN-IN OR RUN-OUT

SEASONS

Bream **Feb.– May**
Dusky flathead & flounder **Nov.– Apr.**
Sand whiting **Oct.– Apr.**
Leatherjacket, mullet, squid & yellowtail **Year round**
Pan sized snapper **Winter**
Silver trevally **Mar.– June**
Mulloway **Oct.– May**

This point is situated in the Garigal National Park and it would take you about 45 mins to and hour to walk to this spot. Once there you will find a rocky outcrop around the point from which you can cast a line or two.

TACTICS

It is my suggestion that you break out the three to three and a half metre rods, spool them up with six kilo line and bring them down to this spot. The tide does move very quickly around here at times, so I would suggest that you use either a ¼ ounce to half ounce star or snapper on a paternoster rig. This will allow the sinker to keep it on the bottom, while letting the baited two hook rig move freely around with the current. You could also try rigging up an outfit with large paddled tail soft plastics and casting up current. This method will allow you to work them slowly back down with the current. Much the same way as you would normally work them on a breakwall.

BAITS AND LURES

Great place to work lures from. I have found it to be mainly a bait fishing area. Try baits, like pink nipper, blood worms, pillie tails and strips of mullet and slimy mackerel. Peeled prawns would also work here, but remember to put a couple of half hitches around the tail of the prawn to stop it flying off when you cast.

BEST TIDE/TIMES

I have found that this spot fish's very well just after there has been a southerly blow and the tide is rising. The bream, flathead and whiting seem to come in closer to feed under the cover of darkness. You can fish here on a run-out tide, but you will need to cast out further to avoid the snags that are in close to the shore.

AMENITIES

None that I know of.

KIDS AND FAMILIES

Fish, fish and more fishing. That's about it.

DAVIDSON PICNIC AREA – MIDDLE HARBOUR

🔍 HOW TO GET THERE

From Wakehurst Parkway turn left into Warringah Road. Travel for about 5 km and turn off left to the Healey toll booth. Pay your parking fee at the toll booth then turn right and follow the road to the end. From here the Lyre Bird walking track takes you to as many landbased fishing spots as you want.

ABOVE: *There is plenty of scenic waterfront access for shorebased anglers.*

🔍 SNAPSHOT

Platform
ROCK WALLS, ESTUARY ROCKS AND SANDY BEACHES

Target species
MULLOWAY
BREAM
DUSKY FLATHEAD
SAND WHITING
LEATHERJACKETS
YELLOWTAIL
SILVER TREVALLY
PAN SIZE SNAPPER
TAILOR
FLOUNDER

Best baits
SQUID, MULLET, PINK NIPPER, BLOOD WORMS

Best lures
SOFT PLASTICS, BLADES

Best time
TOP OF THE TIDE, EITHER RUN-IN OR RUN-OUT

SEASONS

Bream **Feb.– May**
Dusky flathead **Nov.– Apr.**
Sand whiting **Oct.– Apr.**
Leatherjacket & yellowtail **Year round**
Pan sized snapper **Nov.– April**
Silver trevally **Mar.– June**
Flounder **Nov.– April**
Mulloway **Oct.– May**

RIGHT: *You can drive your car to within a short walk to the water.*

If you're after a beautiful waterside setting for a great day out with family or friends, Davidson Park picnic area is perfect, and just a short drive from the Sydney CBD. Large open grassy areas, free BBQs and a stunning Middle Harbour Creek backdrop make this spot the perfect place to unwind. Eucalyptus trees are abundant here, so there's plenty of shade, and lots of space for family games.

TACTICS

Fish in close with a stemmed float for luderick. You need to berley to keep them around your float. You will need to find either green weed or cabbage elsewhere and bring it in with you as there is very little on the rocks. A decent cast from here will get you out into mulloway, kingfish, tailor, salmon, bream and flathead territory. On the run-in tide you could move around the point and fish on the upstream side of the point for bream, trevally, snapper and flathead. The water depth here is about nine to ten metres.

BAITS AND LURES

Surface poppers and large soft plastics can be worked here either early in the morning or just before the sun sets. When there has been a lot of fresh water from a flood you could try using those floating deep divers for a mulloway or two. Half and one ounce blades can be hopped over the bottom here, but you will need to judge it right when you make the last lift as you can easily get snagged up close into the rocks.

BEST TIDE/TIMES

You will find that the eastern side of this point is fished the most. Therefore the run-out tide would be the best time to fish from here as your baits and rigs will stay away from the snags that are in close. During the cooler months of the year the luderick will school up here and quite often it can be shoulder-to-shoulder fishing when they're on the chew.

AMENITIES

BBQ area, car parking (fee applies), cleaning table, plenty of shading trees and picnic tables.

KIDS AND FAMILIES

Great place to bring the family for a day. A place where you can fish while watching the world go by.

MANLY DAM — MANLY

HOW TO GET THERE

Travel north on Spit Road across the Spit Bridge and this will turn into Manly Road, and then into the Burnt Bridge Creek Deviation. On reaching the lights at Condamine Street veer left. Travel about 1 km and then turn left into King Street at Manly Vale. Follow this road to the parking area at the end of this road.

ABOVE: *Manly Dam has a lot on offer for the shore based angler. It just means you may have to do a bit of walking.*

LEFT: *Work the weed beds for bass in the dam.*

SNAPSHOT

Platform
GRASSED AREAS, ROCK WALLS

Target species
BASS
MULLET
SILVER PERCH
CARP
REDFIN

Best baits
WORMS,
BREAD AND
MULLET

Best lures
SURFACE
POPPERS, SOFT
PLASTICS, DIVING
HARDBODIED
LURES

Best time
ALL DAY

SEASONS

Bass **Summer months**
Bream **Feb.– May**
Mullet **Year round**
Silver perch
Year round
Carp **Year round**
Redfin **Year round**

Whether you want to mountain bike, water ski or spend quality time with family and friends by the water, the Manly Warringah War Memorial Park (Manly Dam) has something for everyone. Gates are currently open from 7am to 8.30pm. Manly Dam is popular with novice fishers. Section 4 near the wetlands is thought to be the best fishing spot. The dam is stocked regularly with Australian bass; however other species that may be caught are silver perch, carp and redfin.

TACTICS

It is well documented that bass like erratic retrieves. This cannot be over emphasised. A high majority of surface strikes can be on the splash down or on the first movement after that, or soon after if the lure is in the right place and isn't taken away immediately. Cast your surface lure and let it sit until the rings around it have dissipated. Then give it a single twitch no matter what your lure type. If there is no action at this point then work the lure back. Fishing with surface lures can be one of the most exciting ways of catching bass. There's little to compare with the sound of a strike with the feel of your line going

tight a moment later. It's definitely my favourite form of bass fishing.

BAITS AND LURES

Poppers usually have a flat or slightly cupped face. Usually used for a constant or faster retrieve across the water using the rod to give added animation. Bloopers have a deeper cup than poppers. When twitched they will commonly give off a 'bloop' sound. Best used in small twitches with many pauses.

BEST TIDE/TIMES

Early morning and late afternoons would be the best time to fish here, but you will have to work within the opening and closing times.

AMENITIES

Manly Dam has four picnic areas. To book a picnic table call 9942 2545 or 9942 2640. Visitors can enjoy many activities including swimming, kayaking, fishing, bushwalking, mountain biking, bird watching and waterskiing. There is also a children's playground. The section of water between picnic areas 2 and 3 is a dedicated waterskiing area and is prohibited for swimming and non-motorised water activities. Please use designated swimming areas indicated by buoys and signs.

KIDS AND FAMILIES

Plenty here to keep the kids amused.

🔍 HOW TO GET THERE

Once on the Spit Road travel north over the Spit Bridge and this will turn into Manly Road then turn right into Sydney Road. Travel about 4 km then turn right at Pittwater Road. Turn left into Pine Street and either right or left into North or South Steyne. Find a paid parking spot and walk to the beach.

🔍 SNAPSHOT

Platform
OCEAN BEACH AND ROCKS

Target species
MULLOWAY
BREAM
FLATHEAD
SAND WHITING
SILVER TREVALLY
TAILOR
AUSTRALIAN SALMON
DART

Best baits
BEACH AND BLOOD WORMS, PINK NIPPERS, MULLET, PRAWNS, PILCHARDS, GARFISH, LIVE BAIT

Best lures
METAL SLICES

Best time
ALL DAY

SEASONS

Bream **Feb.– May**
Flathead **Nov.– Apr.**
Sand whiting **Oct.– Apr.**
Silver trevally **Mar.– June**
Flounder **Nov.– April**
Salmon **Mar.– June**
Tailor **Mar.– Aug.**
Mulloway **Oct.– May**

ABOVE: *The parking along this stretch of coastline can be a bit of a nightmare, so be prepared to do a bit of walking to find a productive gutter.*

RIGHT: *The eastern wirrah can be a bit of a by-catch when fishing off the rocks at the southern end of Manly Beach.*

Manly Beach is situated in Sydney's Northern Beaches. From north to south, the three main sections are Queenscliff, North Steyne, and South Steyne. Within walking distance of Manly Beach along the ocean way is Fairy Bower and Shelley Beach. There are shops, restaurants, night clubs and bars in town.

TACTICS

Whenever I am fishing off the beach I always have some kind of bait bucket strapped to one side of my waste and a berley bucket on the other. I tend to use chopped up pilchards and every now and then I throw a handful as far out into the surf as I can get. Sand whiting and mullet are usually the first fish to start to forage up in the shallower areas of the beach. This will start to happen when the water starts to flood over sand spits and bars and right at your feet at the water's edge. You will also find that the movement of the waves will dislodge some of these creatures ready for the whiting to pounce on. The sand whiting will also tend to be one of the last to leave these areas as well, making them easy prey for the larger fish species that will patrol the deep parts of the beach looking for a feed.

BAITS AND LURES

After spending about 2 hours talking to Les from Aquabait, I discovered that not only are tube worms bred for bait that anglers throughout Australia can use, they are also used as food to feed to pregnant prawns in a prawn hatchery and aquarium fish. These amazing worms can be found naturally in up to 60 m of water off the coast from Brisbane in the north and south along the coast through NSW, Victoria, SA and right up to Broome in WA. Where blood worms live in low oxygenated water and mud, the tube worm prefers to live in much cleaner water and sand. The same areas as beach worms.

BEST TIDE/TIMES

All day but best fishing occurs around tide changes around dawn and dusk.

AMENITIES

There aren't any in the immediate area.

KIDS AND FAMILIES

Beaches are always a great place to bring the family and this beach is as great as the rest. Not only can you go fishing here you could also go for a walk or just kick a footy around.

CURL CURL BEACH

RIGHT: *Clear water will also produce the odd ray or two.*

HOW TO GET THERE

Go north on Spit Road over Spit Bridge. This will turn into Manly Road and then into the Burnt Bridge Creek Deviation which turns into Condamine Street. Turn right into William Street, left into Harboard Road, and right into Brighton Street. Travel about 500 m and turn left into Bennett Adams Street. Go down to Griffin Parade, find a parking spot in the Richie Roberts Reserve. It is a short five minute walk to the beach.

ABOVE: *Late afternoon or early mornings are prime times to chase bream from Curl Curl Beach.*

Curl Curl Beach is located on Sydney's northern beaches between Dee Why Beach and Freshwater Beach. It is mainly frequented by locals, so it doesn't get nearly as busy as some of its neighbouring beaches. The beach is approximately 1.1 km long and is divided into North Curl Curl and South Curl Curl. Both ends of the beach have their own surf life saving club, car park and café/kiosk. You will also find rock pools, which are ideal if you want to swim laps or have young children who are not confident swimmers.

TACTICS

When beach fishing the most thing that I state to other anglers is to be patient. Most of all you need to be patient when chasing any fish species. For example, if you strike too soon when you see the down of the float when fishing for luderick you most probably will miss the fish and sometimes if you don't strike soon enough when chasing mulloway you could also miss that fish of a lifetime. Then on the other hand if you are fishing for bream and they are very finicky in the way that they are biting, you may have to not strike and let the fish take the bait down. Now the key to any angler's success is if you can interlock all of these steps together when chasing the fish that you are targeting you too will be able to put yourself up amongst that 10 per cent of anglers who catch 90 per cent of the fish.

BAITS AND LURES

Pipis are found on most longer ocean beaches. They are usually seen when the wave is either coming up the beach or receding down it. The pipis will rise up to the top layer of the sand looking for any small morsel that may pass by. They will also use the motion of the waves to move up and down, as well as along the beach. Once you have located one you will usually find a group of them. Once located all you have to do is the pipi twist with your feet until you feel the hard shell of one. Then it is a matter of leaning down and picking it up out of the sand.

BEST TIDE/TIMES

As with most beaches that are located in Sydney you wouldn't find me fishing them when there is a huge swell running, but you would find me there a couple of days after it has passed through and the seas have settled down.

AMENITIES

At this beach you will find great facilities including toilets, showers, change rooms and bubblers, BBQs and a small playground. There are nearby shops that you can get a drink or a feed from.

KIDS AND FAMILIES

Beaches are always a great places for famiies and this beach is as great as the rest. Not only to fish but also to go for a walk or just kick a footy around.

SNAPSHOT

Platform
OCEAN BEACH AND ROCKS

Target species
MULLOWAY
BREAM
FLATHEAD
SAND WHITING
SILVER TREVALLY
TAILOR
AUSTRALIAN SALMON
DART

Best baits
BEACH AND BLOOD WORMS, PINK NIPPERS, MULLET, PRAWNS, PILCHARDS, GARFISH, LIVE BAIT

Best lures
METAL SLICES

Best time
ALL DAY

SEASONS
Bream **Feb.– May**
Dusky flathead **Nov.– Apr.**
Sand whiting **Oct.– Apr.**
Silver trevally **Mar.– June**
Flounder **Nov.– April**
Salmon **Mar.– June**
Tailor **Mar.– Aug.**
Mulloway **Oct.– May**

NORTH & SOUTH BONDI BEACH

HOW TO GET THERE

Once on Moore Park Road at Paddington travel east until you turn right into Oxford Street. Continue along Oxford Street, which will turn into Einfeld Drive. At the junction of Old South Head Road get into Bondi Road and follow it to the coast. Find paid parking. It is a short walk to the beach.

SNAPSHOT

Platform
OCEAN BEACH AND ROCKS

Target species
MULLOWAY
BREAM
FLATHEAD
SAND WHITING
SILVER TREVALLY
TAILOR
AUSTRALIAN SALMON
LUDERICK
SQUID
DART

Best baits
BEACH AND BLOOD WORMS, PINK NIPPERS, MULLET, PRAWNS, PILCHARDS, GARFISH, LIVE BAIT

Best lures
METAL SLICES

Best time
ALL DAY

SEASONS
Bream **Feb.– May**
Dusky flathead **Nov.– Apr.**
Sand whiting **Oct.– Apr.**
Silver trevally & salmon **Mar.– June**
Tailor **Mar.– Aug.**
Mulloway **Oct.– May**
Luderick **Mar.–Sep.**
Mullet **Year round**
Squid **Year round**

ABOVE: *This low tide gutter would be a great place to start on a rising tide for bream and whiting.*

LEFT: *The rock platform at the southern end of Bondi produces luderick after a southerly blow.*

This popular stretch of water is most popular with tourists and surfers alike but some good fishing can be had along here for those who employ the right techniques.

TACTICS

While bream and whiting can be found just about anywhere in the surf zone at most parts of the day, the prime place to hunt them is along the edges of deep holes and gutters. Now these deep holes and gutters can be found anywhere along the beach and many anglers will cast straight out into the deepest part of the hole or gutter. What I find is that the bream and whiting will tend to just hang off the sand spit or bar, waiting for any tasty morsel to be washed into the hole or gutter. This is where you need to cast your rig, up onto the shallow part and let it be washed back into the hole or gutter with the motion of the waves or current. Now if it is a low tide hole or gutter you will need to concentrate you efforts at the bottom of the tide and if it is a high tide gutter you will need to work the top of the tide.

BAITS AND LURES

As with most beaches that are located in Sydney you wouldn't find me fishing them when there is a huge swell running, but you would find me there a couple of days after it has passed through and the seas have settled down.

AMENITIES

At this beach you will find great facilities including toilets, showers, change rooms and bubblers, BBQs and a small playground. There are nearby shops that you can get a drink or a feed at.

KIDS AND FAMILIES

Beaches are always a great place to bring the family and this beach is as great as the rest. Not only can you go fishing here you could also go for a walk or just kick a footy around.

NORTH BRONTE BEACH

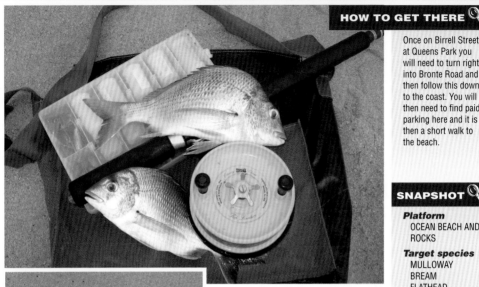

HOW TO GET THERE

Once on Birrell Street at Queens Park you will need to turn right into Bronte Road and then follow this down to the coast. You will then need to find paid parking here and it is then a short walk to the beach.

ABOVE: *A shoulder bag, small tackle, a side cast reel and rod is all you need when chasing bream off the beach.*

LEFT: *The Pflueger Abor reel made all the difference when casting lightly weighted baits off the beach.*

SNAPSHOT

Platform
OCEAN BEACH AND ROCKS

Target species
MULLOWAY
BREAM
FLATHEAD
SAND WHITING
SILVER TREVALLY
TAILOR
AUSTRALIAN SALMON
LUDERICK
SQUID
DART

Best baits
BEACH AND BLOOD WORMS, PINK NIPPERS, MULLET, PRAWNS, PILCHARDS, GARFISH, LIVE BAIT

Best lures
METAL SLICES

Best time
ALL DAY

SEASONS

Bream **Feb.– May**
Dusky flathead **Nov.– Apr.**
Sand whiting **Oct.– Apr.**
Silver trevally & salmon **Mar.– June**
Tailor **Mar.– Aug.**
Mulloway **Oct.– May**
Luderick **Mar.–Sep.**
Mullet **Year round**
Squid **Year round**

Bronte Beach is a small but popular recreational beach on Nelson Bay in Bronte. It is two kilometres south of Bondi Beach and north of the much larger Coogee Beach. A long distance ocean swimming event is held every December between Bondi Beach and Bronte. The three beaches are linked by a paved coastal footpath along the rocky cliff tops, much frequented by tourists and local runners and walkers.

TACTICS

Tailor, Australian salmon and mulloway will all work the same areas as bream and whiting, so you can concentrate your times and efforts to around the same time. I find that the best times tend to be when the change of tide occurs either in the early morning or just on or after sunset. This low-light period will entice the tailor, Australian salmon and mulloway to come in closer to the shore in search of their prey. During the brighter part of the day the Australian salmon and tailor will usually move out to the reefs to rest up, ready to feed at dusk or dawn.

BAITS AND LURES

Try using strips of mullet, whole and half pilchards, pink nippers, beach and blood worms. Don't forget to try those pipis either.

BEST TIDE/TIMES

As with most beaches that are located in Sydney you wouldn't find me fishing them when there is a huge swell running, but you would find me there a couple of days after it has passed through and the seas have settled down. As with many beaches, those early mornings when the sun is rising in your face or when you can feel the last rays of the sun hitting the back of your neck. Winter time is also a great time to fish off the beach, as there are not as many people out and about.

AMENITIES

At this beach you will find great facilities including toilets, showers, change rooms and bubblers, BBQs and a small playground. There are nearby shops that you can get a drink or a feed from.

KIDS AND FAMILIES

Beaches are always a great place to bring the family and this beach is as great as the rest. Not only can you go fishing here, you can also go for a walk or just kick a footy around.

FISHING KNOTS

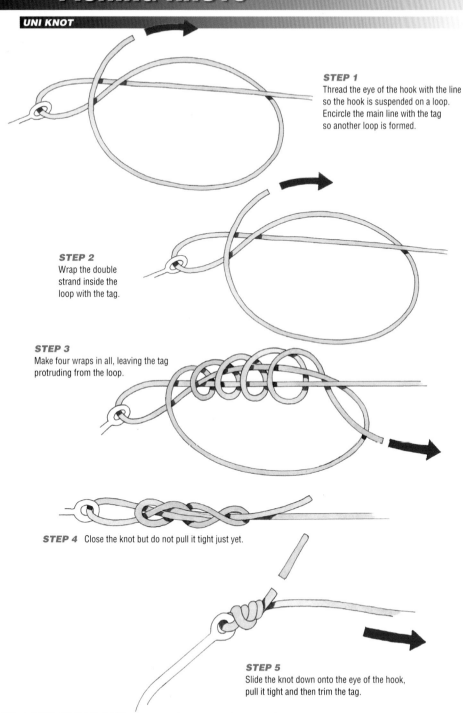

STEP 1
Thread the eye of the hook with the line so the hook is suspended on a loop. Encircle the main line with the tag so another loop is formed.

STEP 2
Wrap the double strand inside the loop with the tag.

STEP 3
Make four wraps in all, leaving the tag protruding from the loop.

STEP 4 Close the knot but do not pull it tight just yet.

STEP 5
Slide the knot down onto the eye of the hook, pull it tight and then trim the tag.

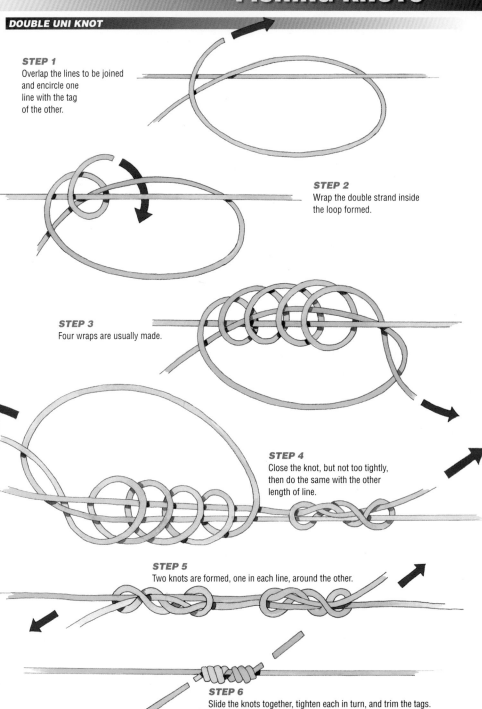

STEP 1
Overlap the lines to be joined and encircle one line with the tag of the other.

STEP 2
Wrap the double strand inside the loop formed.

STEP 3
Four wraps are usually made.

STEP 4
Close the knot, but not too tightly, then do the same with the other length of line.

STEP 5
Two knots are formed, one in each line, around the other.

STEP 6
Slide the knots together, tighten each in turn, and trim the tags.

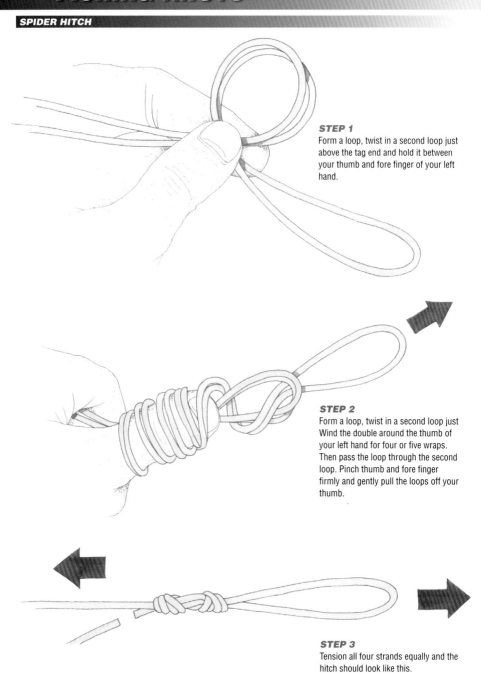

STEP 1

Form a loop, twist in a second loop just above the tag end and hold it between your thumb and fore finger of your left hand.

STEP 2

Form a loop, twist in a second loop just Wind the double around the thumb of your left hand for four or five wraps. Then pass the loop through the second loop. Pinch thumb and fore finger firmly and gently pull the loops off your thumb.

STEP 3

Tension all four strands equally and the hitch should look like this.

FLOATING LIVE BAIT

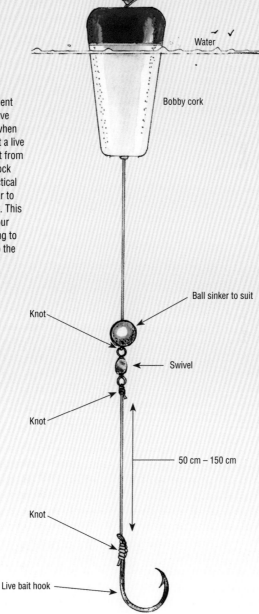

2 x Plastic float stoppers

Main line

Water

Bobby cork

There is often a requirement to position a live bait above the bottom: this occurs when there is a need to present a live bait naturally or to keep it from swimming into bottom rock and weed. The most practical way to fish a live bait near to surface is beneath a float. This rig will satisfy most of your requirements when aiming to present a live bait near to the surface.

Knot

Ball sinker to suit

Swivel

Knot

50 cm – 150 cm

Knot

Live bait hook

PATERNOSTER RIG FOR ESTUARY, ROCK & BEACH

The paternoster rig is used widely in fishing circles. The reason for this is that it is an effective rig for presenting a bait immediately above the bottom. In the event that the bottom provides weed and rock snags, the paternoster rig will enable you to keep a bait above such threats. Waters that offer current such as those in the beach environment are often best fished using a paternoster rig.

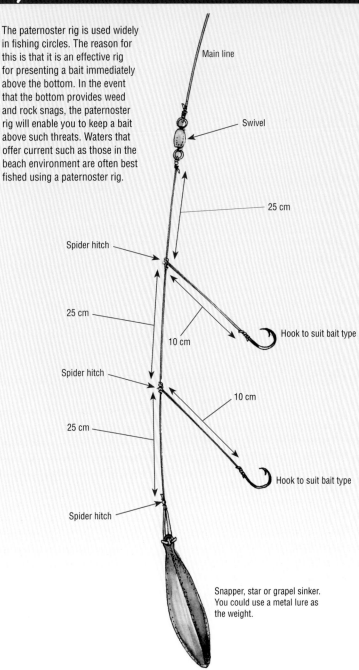

Main line

Swivel

25 cm

Spider hitch

25 cm

10 cm

Hook to suit bait type

Spider hitch

10 cm

25 cm

Hook to suit bait type

Spider hitch

Snapper, star or grapel sinker. You could use a metal lure as the weight.

A running rig is one of the simplest rigs to produce but is often very snag-resistant and deadly on fish. The ability for a fish to 'run' with a bait without feeling too much resistance will often fool cautious feeders. The impact of running a sinker immediately on top of the hook reduces the potential for snagging of the rig. Use just enough weight to get your bait to the depth of the fish and you will be catching them in no time.

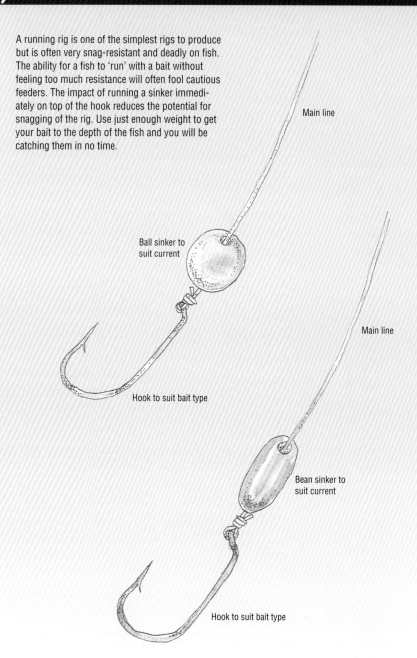

Main line

Ball sinker to suit current

Main line

Hook to suit bait type

Bean sinker to suit current

Hook to suit bait type

BAIT PRESENTATION

SLIDING SNOOD FOR STRIP BAIT

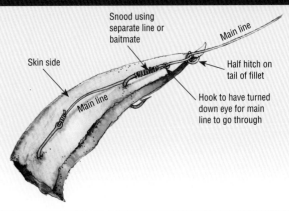

Snood using separate line or baitmate

Main line

Skin side

Half hitch on tail of fillet

Hook to have turned down eye for main line to go through

Main line

SLIDING SNOOD FOR LIVE BAIT

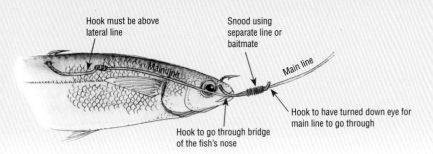

Hook must be above lateral line

Snood using separate line or baitmate

Main line

Main line

Hook to have turned down eye for main line to go through

Hook to go through bridge of the fish's nose

WORMS 1

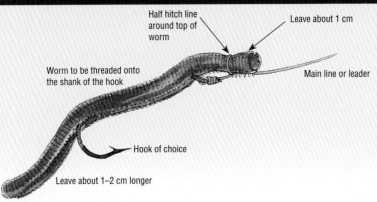

Half hitch line around top of worm

Leave about 1 cm

Worm to be threaded onto the shank of the hook

Main line or leader

Hook of choice

Leave about 1–2 cm longer

BAIT PRESENTATION

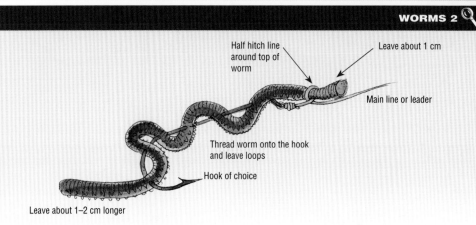

Half hitch line around top of worm

Leave about 1 cm

Main line or leader

Thread worm onto the hook and leave loops

Hook of choice

Leave about 1–2 cm longer

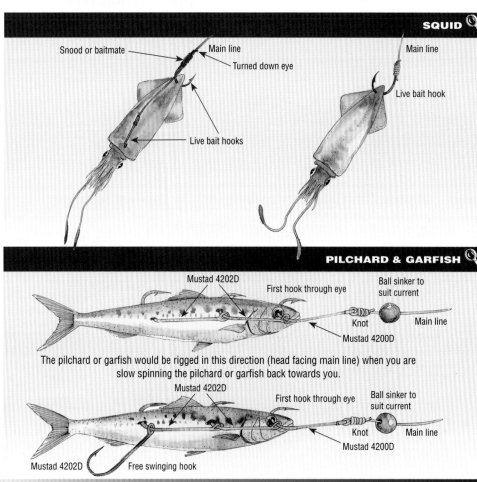

Snood or baitmate

Main line

Turned down eye

Live bait hooks

Main line

Live bait hook

Mustad 4202D

First hook through eye

Ball sinker to suit current

Knot

Main line

Mustad 4200D

The pilchard or garfish would be rigged in this direction (head facing main line) when you are slow spinning the pilchard or garfish back towards you.

Mustad 4202D

First hook through eye

Ball sinker to suit current

Knot

Main line

Mustad 4200D

Mustad 4202D

Free swinging hook

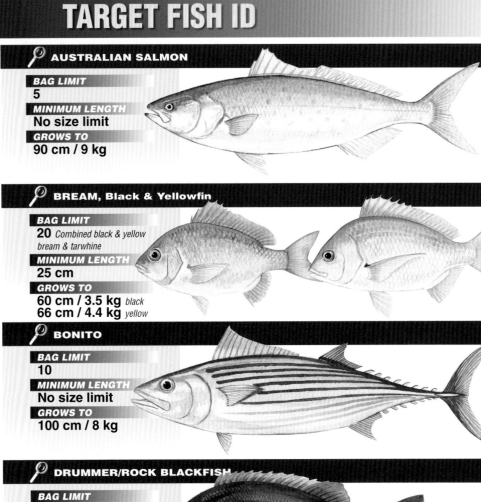

AUSTRALIAN SALMON

BAG LIMIT
5

MINIMUM LENGTH
No size limit

GROWS TO
90 cm / 9 kg

BREAM, Black & Yellowfin

BAG LIMIT
20 Combined black & yellow
bream & tarwhine

MINIMUM LENGTH
25 cm

GROWS TO
60 cm / 3.5 kg black
66 cm / 4.4 kg yellow

BONITO

BAG LIMIT
10

MINIMUM LENGTH
No size limit

GROWS TO
100 cm / 8 kg

DRUMMER/ROCK BLACKFISH

BAG LIMIT
10

MINIMUM LENGTH
30 cm

GROWS TO
75 cm / 8 kg

DUSKY FLATHEAD

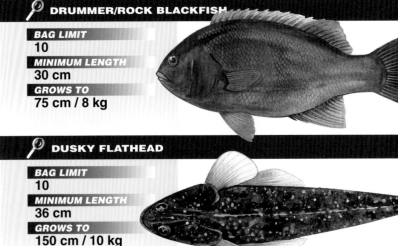

BAG LIMIT
10

MINIMUM LENGTH
36 cm

GROWS TO
150 cm / 10 kg

No more than
1 fish over 70 cm.

FLOUNDER

BAG LIMIT
20 Total for all species including sole

MINIMUM LENGTH
25 cm No size limit for sole

GROWS TO
50 cm / 1 kg

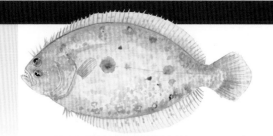

GARFISH

BAG LIMIT
20

MINIMUM LENGTH
No size limit

GROPER, Blue, Brown, Red

BAG LIMIT
2 Only 1 over 60 cm

MINIMUM LENGTH
30 cm

GROWS TO
120 cm / 30 kg

LEATHERJACKETS

BAG LIMIT
20 Total for all leatherjackets

MINIMUM LENGTH
No size limit

GROWS TO
35 cm

LUDERICK

BAG LIMIT
20 Total for all leatherjackets

MINIMUM LENGTH
27 cm

GROWS TO
70 cm / 4.5 kg

TARGET FISH ID

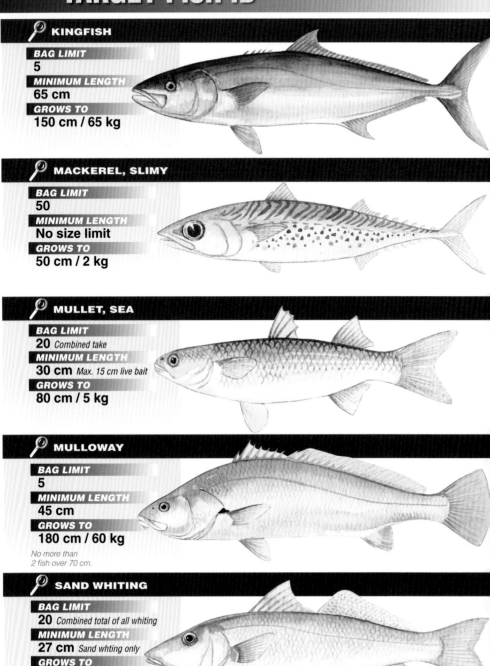

KINGFISH

BAG LIMIT
5

MINIMUM LENGTH
65 cm

GROWS TO
150 cm / 65 kg

MACKEREL, SLIMY

BAG LIMIT
50

MINIMUM LENGTH
No size limit

GROWS TO
50 cm / 2 kg

MULLET, SEA

BAG LIMIT
20 Combined take

MINIMUM LENGTH
30 cm Max. 15 cm live bait

GROWS TO
80 cm / 5 kg

MULLOWAY

BAG LIMIT
5

MINIMUM LENGTH
45 cm

GROWS TO
180 cm / 60 kg

No more than
2 fish over 70 cm.

SAND WHITING

BAG LIMIT
20 Combined total of all whiting

MINIMUM LENGTH
27 cm Sand whting only

GROWS TO
47 cm / 1 kg

TARGET FISH ID

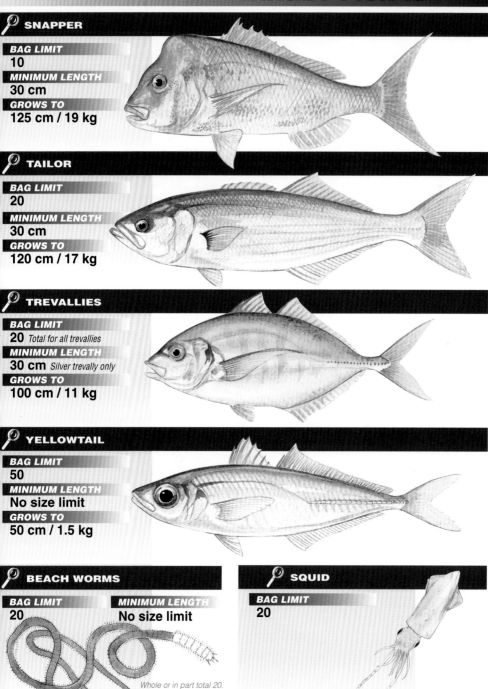

SNAPPER
BAG LIMIT
10
MINIMUM LENGTH
30 cm
GROWS TO
125 cm / 19 kg

TAILOR
BAG LIMIT
20
MINIMUM LENGTH
30 cm
GROWS TO
120 cm / 17 kg

TREVALLIES
BAG LIMIT
20 *Total for all trevallies*
MINIMUM LENGTH
30 cm *Silver trevally only*
GROWS TO
100 cm / 11 kg

YELLOWTAIL
BAG LIMIT
50
MINIMUM LENGTH
No size limit
GROWS TO
50 cm / 1.5 kg

BEACH WORMS
BAG LIMIT
20

MINIMUM LENGTH
No size limit

*Whole or in part total 20.
All other worms 100
combined total.*

SQUID
BAG LIMIT
20

TARGET FISH ID

BAG LIMIT
2 *(4 possession) combined bass/*
estuary perch; only 1 (inc. 1 pos-
session) over 35 cm in rivers

GROWS TO
65 cm / 4 kg

Possession limit 1 over   *Bass closed season 1 June –*
35 cm *in rivers*   *31 August (rivers/estuary)*

🔍 **PERCH, ESTUARY**

BAG LIMIT
2 *(4 possession) combined bass/*
estuary perch; only 1 (inc. 1 pos-
session) over 35 cm in rivers

GROWS TO
65 cm / 7.5 kg

Only 1 over **35 cm** *in rivers*

🔍 **PERCH, GOLDEN**

BAG LIMIT
5 *Daily (10 possession)*

MINIMUM LENGTH
30 cm

GROWS TO
70 cm / 15 kg

🔍 **PERCH, SILVER**

BAG LIMIT
5 *in listed dams*

MINIMUM LENGTH
25 cm

GROWS TO
60 cm / 8 kg

(10 possession in listed dams)
NO TAKE RIVERS

🔍 **REDFIN**

BAG LIMIT
No bag limit

MINIMUM LENGTH
No size limit

REELS, RODS &
ACCESSORIES

ENSURE A GREAT DAYS